AF316703

EVERYBODY CAN'T GO

STEPHANIE JESSICA HOLLEY

ALSO BY STEPHANIE JESSICA HOLLEY

WRITE THE VISION, MAKE IT PLAIN
An Everybody Can't Go Journal

Learning Yourself Workbook

WRITE THE VISION, MAKE IT PLAIN: Updated & Expanded
An Everybody Can't Go Journal

Re-Write the Vision: RESET & Realign
An Everybody Can't Go Journal

Everybody Can't Go

There's Less Space At Your Next Level

Stephanie Jessica Holley, M.S. Ed

Copyright 2025 by Stephanie Jessica Holley

All rights reserved.
Published in the United States by Ingram Spark

Library of Congress Cataloging-in-Publication Data is available upon request.

ISBN
Ebook ISBN

Printed in the United States of America

Book design by Stephanie Jessica Holley
Jacket design by Stephanie Jessica Holley

10 9 8 7 6 5 4 3 2 1

First Edition

DEDICATION

This book is dedicated to every courageous person who has made a commitment to personal growth and experienced the loss that comes with becoming the best version of you.

TABLE OF CONTENTS

FOREWORD

Listen to me carefully: when somebody writes directly from their calling, it just feels different. You don't have to guess where it's coming from. The message comes alive. That's exactly what you'll experience reading *Everybody Can't Go*. It's obvious Jessica didn't write this book to make a name for herself. I'm not saying anything would be wrong with that. But she was being obedient to God. She made peace with the consequences of obedience before she ever invited us into her process. That's what makes this book so dope. Can I be honest? There is a lot of theory out there. This ain't that. This ain't AI. I can tell she put in the work and she earned wisdom through personal growth.

Most people don't talk openly about that space between knowing what God said and actually doing it. I have been telling the world that I am a recovering people pleaser. It was a blindspot for me for years. I kept certain people in my circle longer than I should have because I made decisions based on emotion instead of alignment. In the beginning, when C.J. looked me in the face and said he was going to make me a household name, I assumed everybody with us then would be with us now. That didn't happen. Some people stopped growing. I tried to hold on longer than I should have. I convinced myself that loyalty required lifelong access, but that wasn't the truth. When I wrote *You Owe You* and it hit the *New York Times* bestseller list, that was the message I wanted everybody to get. Nobody will take care of you better than you. And if you surround yourself with people who feel entitled to your sacrifice but won't match your discipline, you'll lose everything trying to keep them close.

Let me say it again so you can get it: some people tell themselves that just staying connected or being consistent as a sign of loyalty is enough, even when that connection keeps them stuck. Jessica isn't speaking from the safety of hindsight. She said it. That would be too easy. She speaks from her experience of obedience. She's made the hard decisions. But, really, let me say it this way: decisions are just decisions. People make them hard. She made the solid decision that if relationships aren't mutual they can't go. I love it. That is the same decision that made me the number-one motivational speaker in the world and made my marriage blissful. Are you listening?

This book doesn't waste time trying to convince you to move. That wouldn't make sense. It meets you at the moment when you already know you have to. Can I be honest? If you're reading this book, you already know some of the people in your life can't go where you're going. You're not confused right now. You might tell yourself you're confused. The weight you feel is because you're taking too long to make the decision. And what Jessica does with this message is help you see the delay for what it is. She names it. If you're gonna defeat what's standing in your way, you have to call it what it is. She walks through it and removes the emotions that keep people stuck. By the time you finish reading, you'll have to decide if you're going to keep doing what's not working, or finally surround yourself with people that light up when you come in the room and are not just with you for what they can take from you.

I don't put my name on projects unless there's alignment. And I'm telling you Jessica is aligned and her message is aligned. If you're reading it with integrity and you're ready to do the work, your life is about to change, I promise you. You'll be aligned.

God never told you to bring everybody with you. That was your idea. Now it's time to correct it. Get a notebook. Take notes. Tell the truth. And write this down at the top of the page: "Everybody can go!" Now you know. Let's go...

—*Eric Thomas, Ph.D. (E.T. the Hip-Hop Preacher)*

INTRODUCTION

We each have a unique life journey that we move through, learning, developing, and becoming the person we're inspired to be. We were born to love, dream big dreams, and fulfill our purpose, becoming whole. It's a beautiful and adventurous journey full of swings and dips, but then this thing happens...with people. Sometimes, we're born into families that influenced or raised us to stop dreaming "too big"—to stay complacent once we've "done enough" or are doing "better than the next person."

We get unsolicited advice shoved on us about all the reasons why we should stop striving for something better and instead live a life we see as mundane while those around us are happy with where they are in life. We endure backhanded conversations on how much we've changed. We look around at our friends, family, colleagues, and social circles and realize we feel alone or rejected.

This is a long-standing problem for anyone who has made significant improvements to their lives or has considered making such moves and internalized the voices of others around them. When other people's voices become louder than your inner voice and God's voice, the former creates a recipe for disaster as you grow in life and chase after your dreams. You likely find yourself suffocating in a day-to-day routine others want for you, and you don't want that life for yourself. You desire more.

This book's premise is based primarily on my experience and secondarily on the stories others have shared with me on learning how to move forward when relationship conflicts arise during their growth journey. I only wish I had the resources available to me back then that I have now.

Growth includes outgrowing spaces, places you were once comfortable with, and sometimes the people who choose to stay stagnant in those places. Because we're used to our familiar environments and people, we often don't consider the full scope of change that comes with growth, especially if we're making quantum leaps personally, professionally, spiritually, and financially. We also aren't usually prepared for how such exponential growth will impact the social, familial, and romantic aspects of our lives.

Hearing many similar stories made me realize I wasn't the only one. People have shared with me and in groups that they're struggling with elevating to their next level because of things their friends and family say about their journey. I've heard stories of friends and family not saying a thing, then treating the person differently after he or she made significant life changes for the better. Countless people have told me about their growth journey to become their best self, become financially stable, gain opportunities they always dreamed of, while thinking the same friends and family would always be there and even grow with them. We're talking about good-hearted people like you who wanted to bring their loved ones along for more than just the ride, but to bring them along for life.

Some stories were disappointing, some sad, and others downright devastating, but they shared one common thing: These people experienced guilt, grief, and loneliness as they moved forward in the better lives they painstakingly built for themselves.

After hearing my own story reflected onto me so many times, I knew I had to share the message from the other side of these negative feelings. The path may be rocky, but the other side of the mountain is beautiful when you realize you're not alone in this, and that so many amazing things and new people are waiting on that other side of the guilt and grief of letting go.

As you read on, I hope you find comfort in knowing that you're not alone, that it's not always your fault alone, and that there are many others out there like us who've had to learn the life lesson that **everybody can't go.**

INSIGHT AND FORESIGHT: SELF-ASSESSMENT TO DEFINE YOUR LIFE GOALS

Vision

noun
The ability to think about or plan the future with imagination or wisdom.

While the textbook definition of the word vision only talks about thinking and planning, I think the most important part of your vision is *writing it down*. Is it really even a plan if it's not properly documented?

Taking the time to write out (not type) your vision may take 10 minutes, or it could take weeks. New details may come to life for you as you envision the answers to your five W's (who, what, when, where, and why). Writing your vision on paper gives you time to dig as deep as you want and think about what you truly want in life. You'll be forced to *slow down* as you write because your hands can only move so fast as your mind works through all the details and maybe even things you hadn't considered before. For example, say you want a big house. Where? What does it look like? Will it be your forever home? Is this the place you imagine raising your family in? And what does your family look like? You and the dog or kitty, the family you were born into, or the one you're creating? Does the family in your vision contain people you haven't even met yet?

You see how the questions can keep rolling out of a one-line idea? The stream of consciousness connecting one thought to another is exactly why writing your vision is necessary. You can't possibly remember all those details when it's time to make decisions without a reference. Without slowing down to write things down, we'd never get to untangle that long stream of thought with so many related ideas, wants, and needs. Just think of how difficult it would be to explain your vision to another person if you can't make verbal sense of it and understand yourself.

Now consider this: If you can't explain your vision to another person, how do you know if the person belongs in your life as part of that vision?

Growing up in church, I learned Habakkuk 2:2-3, but it wasn't until I was an adult and in a personal development session that I took the directions literally and used it tangibly. The scripture reads:

> *Then the LORD answered me and said: "Write the vision and make it plain on tablets, that he may run who reads it. For the vision is yet for an appointed time; but at the end it will speak, and it will not lie. Though it tarries, wait for it; because it will surely come, it will not tarry.*

Your vision is important because it's the written account of your mental depiction of where you plan to go in life. Thinking through your life's vision and writing it down serves as a springboard for your future planning and a standard from which to compare your life's choices. This written vision can also be a resource for road mapping how you would like to change your life from its current state to what you want it to be. Exploring what you can become, who you can become, and what you can achieve is all part of the process. The vision may be so vivid for you that you can write everything down in one sitting, or, if words or writing aren't your strong suit, you may need a few sessions as you find ways to translate the vision into words on a page. I suggest you find a quiet space where you can be alone without interruption, with time to clear your mind from the daily life clutter, and pray before you begin writing.

Your written vision becomes the framework of your "vision roadmap." Now, this won't be a literal roadmap with cities, states, expressways, and streets on it. This roadmap will contain your instructions, contingencies, deadlines, and milestones for how to achieve your vision. Your vision roadmap will be a reference guide, a reminder of where you're going in life and how you plan to get there. When you're off-track or experience a setback, challenge, or even failure, your vision roadmap is where you'll return to reset, realign, and find another way to move forward and mark your milestones and goals as complete.

Making your vision a reality involves creating a timeline with milestones to measure your progress on your roadmap. Your vision requires a measurement tool to ensure that you are getting there. Whether you're moving faster or slower than you initially intended, make sure you're moving forward. If you have to take a break, pause, or reroute, it helps to know exactly where you left off in order to continue.

While your vision is a plan depicting your ultimate set of goals, it's easier (if I dare to use that word) to get there with a deadline. Deadlines are required to give yourself due dates for completing a certain set of tasks before revising your plans or continuing forward.

Next, you'll need milestones. Group those deadlines and take the time to celebrate your wins, both big and small, along the way. Your roadmap will help you create instructions for yourself to take the small steps that lead to big gains in bringing your vision to life.

Once you're clear on your vision—the what—you can focus on the why. Why do you want the life that you wrote in your vision? This answer will show you what drives you. You can find related sources that inspire you to move forward in life. Finding these sources of energy will serve you well while you begin physically building that vision and bringing the words on paper to life. The journey of tangibly achieving your vision will challenge your mental, emotional, and spiritual states. This is one of many steps in building or repairing your existing foundation, strengthening it so you can move forward.

Goal

noun

plural noun: goals
the object of a person's
ambition or effort; an
aim or desired result.

Goal setting has become the "new wave." It sounds trendy, looks good on social media, or can be made into milestones on the path to your dream life. This depends on your level of commitment, consistency, and effort. Everyone has goals of some sort. There's just a difference in the goals we each set for ourselves. Goals are different from dreams—without a plan in place for achieving said dreams there is no aim or measuring, just wanting.

Because it's currently trendy to portray a larger-than-life existence through social media, there's a new epidemic. Everyone wants to be a game changer in the world, and many people have begun to label themselves as goal-getters and expect recognition for doing the normal actions of "adulting." While there is a targeted group of people who take their goals seriously and have applied a plan and a systemic approach to getting those goals accomplished, there are also those who are internally complacent but use the language of an actual executor to be accepted and masquerade within a group of people who win.

This isn't to push a narrative that accomplishing goals is easy. A lot of time, effort, and startup capital are needed to pursue any plan to accomplish your goals. But every person who gave up on her dream or became complacent along the way isn't a "bad person" or unworthy of connection.

We each have a level of ambition to achieve our wildest dreams. Depending on the path we've followed, many circumstances can cause us to let our goals or dreams die as we get older. When they do, our ambition changes course, and we focus on something else.

With goal setting becoming more of a trend than an action plan over the past decade, I've experienced four general categories of behavior when it comes to the actual lifestyle of goal setters:

1. Oblivious Lifers
2. Complacent Talkers
3. Pump Fake Goalers
4. Ambition Drivers
5. Goal Getters

Oblivious Lifers have no clue what is at the next level and no desire to learn or find out what other options are available to them in life. These people have no ambition or drive to aspire to something new, different, or outside their current norm.

Complacent Talkers are satisfied with where they are in life and will do nothing additional to build themselves or grow to the next level. While they have the potential to do so, they have no drive, ambition, or desire to become any more than what they currently are, despite the opportunities available to them. These people refuse to do the work to better themselves and are content with their current circumstances enough to stay there. While they might think about it or desire more, they refuse to *do* anything to drive themselves toward improvement or personal growth.

Some of these individuals will go so far as to learn the language of goal-oriented people to fit in and masquerade among the crowd or social circle. They have no problem conversing about ideas, think-tanking, or engaging in roundtable discussions on plans that they will never participate in beyond the conversation at hand. This is damaging to others. Look out for those who take up space but have no plans of truly contributing to a common goal.

If we don't guard our goal and vision, the Complacent Talker can latch on, undetected for a year or two (in some cases even longer), before we realize the growth they so eloquently spoke about was just that—only talk. They have no action behind it that leads to tangible results. This type of person becomes evident over time, and when the promise of growth doesn't happen, the dynamic between the two (or more) of you may be damaged because that person isn't truthful in her intentions of keeping your company and ends up wasting your resources without producing.

Contributing factors and characteristics of these individuals include (but are not limited to):

- **Comfort with the current situation:** A stable job, the feeling of security in a loose routine, and a sense of familiarity that discourages them from stepping outside of their comfort zone to grow to their next level in any or limited aspects in life.
- **A paralyzing fear of failure or making mistakes that stops them from taking any risk, large or small.** This includes minimizing or avoiding any steps into new territory, whether physical, spiritual, mental, emotional, or financial.
- **Lack of self-awareness in areas for improvement.** This is what my mentorship calls "the inability to self-assess." People with no awareness of their weaknesses don't know their areas of potential growth. Some even feel like there's no need to improve themselves.
- **External validation from others fulfills their need for praise.** There may be people-pleasing mixed in here, with meeting others' expectations rather than focusing on their own goals. This distracts them from building themselves and garners more praise from others by *seeming* to do more than they truly produce.
- **Low self-esteem** causes them to doubt their capabilities and underestimate their potential, leading to stagnation.
- **They have no goals set, therefore no life roadmap,** and continue the daily or weekly cycle of mundane tasks, simply existing.

Complacency can come from a combination of the factors above and other factors not previously mentioned, like familial teachings and values, economic status, education level (all forms of exposure, not just formal degrees), and mindset.

If any of this sounds like you, and you want to overcome being a Complacent Talker, the first thing you need is true self-reflection. Ask yourself, *why do I carry on this way? What's stopping me from growing into the best version of myself?* Next, build self-confidence, find a powerful "why," set goals that align with what you truly want, and finally, execute one step at a time to achieve the established goal.

Pump Fake Goalers are those who take complacent talking a bit further. They showboat around social and business circles with a great story of what they're *about* to do. "I'm starting this new business....", "I'm making investments....and getting money....", "I'm building a team..." and the list goes on. These sentence fragments are great for telling your story or segueing into conversations to share what you're currently doing and to reach out to others who can be an active part of your wins. But here's the thing about Pump Fake Goalers: They never actually produce. They come around with an amazing story just to be around, gain acceptance, see what resources they can siphon out of others, and never really multiply the resources they're given. "Well, I'm 'bout to...." "I'm gonna..." "I'm finna..." "I was gonna..."

Ambition Drivers have the potential to do great things and use some of their resources to achieve some level of success. They're great at encouraging others to pursue their passions and work progressively toward building the life they want. Ambition Drivers can keep company with most because of their giving nature, cheerful demeanor, and positive encouragement toward others. They help others as well as themselves.

Goal Getters are the achievers who take the resources available to them, multiply them, and get a return—and not just financially. They use self-improvement, learning opportunities, and knowledge to assess and refine how to accomplish their goals.

Goal Getters have written a vision, decided milestones, created a plan, and actively executed it, yielding tangible results. These people grow over time; others can see the fruits of their labor, and they continue to be lifelong learners. They find ways to work smarter, not harder, as they progress in life. These people are often open-minded, giving, and encouraging.

Insight

noun
the capacity to gain an
accurate and deep
intuitive understanding
of a person or thing.

We often want to gain insight into people, situations, or concepts and seek to learn about a topic, but how often do we turn that curiosity inward and examine ourselves for a deep and accurate understanding of who we are?

In short, how often do you take the time to understand yourself? I mean a truthful, deep examination of your innermost self. How are you truly feeling mentally, emotionally, and spiritually, and why do you feel that way?

You'll need self-assessment for your journey because you must first understand yourself, your wants, your desires, your dreams, your weaknesses, and your strengths to move forward in life in the most fulfilling and powerful ways possible. You must deeply understand yourself before you can truly understand others and how to properly communicate with them. You'll need to understand what drives you, what motivates you, what your ultimate goal in life is. You must decide whether you're willing to make a commitment and work for it day and night in relentless pursuit until you get it done.

Self-awareness is crucial in assessing when to release others from your life. If you don't know yourself first, your decision-making process for allowing others access to your life will be unregulated. This leads to connections with people that may not be good for you and causes you to stagnate in a place in life you were meant to move away from. You'll need insight to help you establish grounds for who you are, your purpose, your vision, and creating your plan to get it done.

Self-awareness will make you more intentional as you formulate your milestones and roadmap. You'll more accurately determine how far you can push yourself in accomplishing your milestones and know when to adjust when faced with uncontrollable circumstances and individuals who disrupt your work.

Vision = Dream + Plan

Milestones (Timeline)
+ Execution &
Consistency =
Guaranteed Growth

Foresight

noun

the ability to predict or the action of predicting what will happen or be needed in the future.

Looking forward in your life requires foresight. You won't be able to look ahead, make predictions, or plan for future needs if you don't know where you're going or what you want. By defining what your vision looks like and writing it down, you have a clear picture of what your next steps in life will be. While we can't tell the future, we can make educated guesses based on currently available evidence to predict our next steps. People leave clues that tell you how they will likely show up for you based upon how they conduct themselves, how they have or have not shown up for others, and how they've shown up for you in the past.

We must maximize foresight when we're predicting what we'll need to accomplish the next goal. Your vision, once written, is just that—a written vision—until you take action to bring the words on the page to life. While you may ask God to bless your vision once you've written it and made it plain, that doesn't mean it comes to fruition by Birtha alone. You're responsible for bringing it to life in the physical realm. This requires resources of many kinds: work, money, people, learning, systems, and more.

Are you serving yourself, and are those surrounding you serving you? Are you allowed the space and trust to pour into them as well? For a moment, take your time and just be. Be alone and find your thoughts without the influence of anyone else's opinions, suggestions, or teachings. Take more time to think about what you want to do with your life if money isn't an object, if you only had to worry about yourself without any responsibility to anyone else. Think of an "if I were king/queen for a year" scenario. Find what truly matters to you and spend the rest of your life building, achieving, and ultimately living that dream. If you've already completed the task of writing down your vision, then this is a helpful exercise to get more details written down and to help in creating attainable milestones.

People are involved at every step of your dream life and vision. Some will come into your life as blessings, some will attach themselves to you for a need, and others will be there to teach you life lessons. It's our responsibility to pay attention to the role others play in achieving our vision. Both positive and negative experiences help us grow into who we are meant to be. Of all relationships, our lifetime relationships are the most important for us to recognize.

And of the lifelong relationships you'll have, the most important person you will ever know in your lifetime is you. Be sure you meet yourself at every stage in life and encourage that version of yourself to keep striving to be the best you that you can be. As you learn to be in a great relationship with yourself, you'll be able to make the best decisions for you and your vision.

Take inventory of the people you spend most of your time with and who you communicate with most often. We all carry habits and mannerisms from the people we spend the most time with. We make memories together, inside jokes, and other bond-building interactions that affect how we think, behave, and contribute to the world. When spending time with others, we can unconsciously internalize their words and behaviors. This could be a positive or negative thing. How many times have you heard this adage or something like it?

"If you're hanging around with four fools, you will certainly be the fifth. If you hang around with four millionaires, you're bound to be the fifth."

Looking at the five people you spend the most time with, ask yourself: *Are they assets or liabilities?* Do the people in your circle do anything to add value to your life or help you become who you need to be to reach your goals and fulfill your vision? Friends should be in your life as support, provide camaraderie, give advice, hold you accountable, learn and grow, provide a listening ear, and be social and business partners.

We often neglect to create friendships with an end goal in mind when it comes to our circle of friends or influence. Everyone who begins your journey with you will not make it to the end with you. If you're convinced that you'll be able to keep everyone as you grow and build toward your vision, then consider a few things:

1. Are you confident because you've already pruned your social network?
2. Are you currently bearing dead weight and have been lucky enough to progress in your plans so far?
3. Have you taken the time to consider your needs, wants, and vision and whether some people need to go?
4. Are you holding on to relationships that are parasitic and draining you, but you've grown used to it?

Some people were meant to begin with you, some to help you along the way, and others to ascend with you to the top in a relationship serving you both. Everyone along the way is not meant to be by your side at all stages or levels, nor is everyone in your circle able to be a constant contributor to your vision without reciprocity on your part. There are levels to this.

"A dream without a
goal and a plan is just a
wish."

My Own Story: Gathering Friends

I began to form my social circle as I started my new journey as a freshman at the University of Detroit Mercy. I was a theater major at a predominantly white Institution (PWI), and it wasn't hard for all the black students to find one another because there weren't many of us in comparison to the full campus population. I met people from different states, other metropolitan areas, and people from different socioeconomic classes than mine.

I made friends with people who were given enough allowance and had their accounts funded so they could walk over to the student accounting office and pay their tuition from their debit card all in one swipe. On the other hand, I was admitted on an academic scholarship that covered the cost of my education based upon the stipulation that I maintain a 3.0 GPA or higher and not ever be placed on academic probation.

Many of the students who attended the university who were also from the inner city of Detroit were admitted through high school programs to help bridge the educational gap left when gaining a high school education at an inner-city school.

We were a melting pot and were able to learn from one another because of our diverse backgrounds. We all started on the same level as freshmen. The upperclassmen saw us and took us under their wings, usually hanging out in the Student Union on campus. We were there to support and help one another in this new transition in life and the upperclassmen were always willing to show us the ropes and encourage us to work together. It was truly a time of living the "we all we got" philosophy and community was at an all-time high. We shared everything from books to meals, cars, and class notes, and created study groups to ensure that we were all able to at least get a B on tests in the classes rumored to be the most academically challenging by the hardest professors.

Because everyone needed some form of support, everyone was willing to pitch in where they had a strength or resource that others could use. Everyone couldn't afford all the textbooks needed for their course load. With books sometimes exceeding $700 per semester at that time, that kind of money just for books was an impossible task for some of us to achieve. We still had to read texts, and still needed to study, so that called for someone with a book, someone with a car, someone with notes and someone with a bit of cash on hand or money on their student ID to provide food.

With several people bringing resources to not only the proverbial table but the actual study table in the basement of that Student Union, we were able to successfully ace most of our exams when we coordinated time management properly and worked together to create a well-oiled machine so that everybody could eat and study.

There was one other junior in the theater program, Sophia, who took me under her wing once she found out I was in the program as well. We quickly became friends, and she helped guide me through the difficulties of being a black woman in theater at the institution and at large. We spent a lot of time together and were as thick as thieves.

I found Liam in my English class and the three of us would commute together to and from school. I met Mia, her roommate Amelia, Emma, and Charlotte in our university's gospel choir and we participated in bible study together. I always brought people together and introduced my friends to one another to make new connections.

As undergrad continued, new freshmen classes entered and now I was a part of the community that set out to mentor and befriend the other black students, showing them the ropes just as I was assimilated during my freshman year.

When I moved onto campus, I became close friends with other transfer students and some of the incoming freshmen. There was always a road trip with my high school friends Violet and Chloe, visiting each other's dorms on my campus or at Michigan State. We went on missions with my friends Olivia and Harper, who I hung out with frequently on campus. With all the partying we did, it's a wonder any of us got any sleep or maintained our GPAs. I had no choice and refused to give up on any part of my experience, so I got used to sleeping 3-5 hours a night so I wouldn't miss any action.

As we continued over the years, I formed a fairly wide social circle from different activities, classes, organizations and extracurriculars. I had multiple friendship groups: my theater buddies, my bible study and Gospel Choir friends, my sorority sisters, and friends from other organizations. As undergrad continued, some of my good friends graduated or moved out of state and we stayed in touch. We shared some of the same goals in life and were still there to encourage one another even though we didn't get to spend as much time together daily. We'd had bonding experiences together and had grown over the years together. We'd supported one another as slowly the initial group of us began to transition to working adulthood and post-college life.

I was still on campus after my older friends graduated. You couldn't find Amelia, Charlotte, Emma, or me in too many places without another one of us being present. We participated in some of the same classes, the same church activities, and the same gospel choir. We shared many moments of spiritual warfare, healing, and learning about God at a deeper level in the company of one another. These were friendships that I just knew would last a lifetime. We started our young adulthood together and made it through some of our toughest times as young adults by leaning on one another. We made plans for life after we graduated, moved into the work world, and "adulting."

Synergy includes the best of what everyone has to offer and brings to the group. Are there people in your circle with nothing to offer—and I mean consistently have nothing to offer to the group—and they're just there? Valuable relationships are about reciprocity, a cycle of you being a valuable person and keeping company with other valuable people. You're each willing and able to pour into each other in different areas of life to help build one another and your bond becomes fortified over time. The amount of time doesn't matter when the quality of the time spent is high.

To be able to provide those in your life with value, you must first know your worth and how you bring value to the table. When we're unaware of the value we carry, we're vulnerable to others misusing us instead of being a useful person and benefiting from reciprocity.

Take time for yourself to learn what makes you a valuable person. Doing so will build your self-assurance in what you have to offer. You'll speak more confidently about the decisions that lead to your vision because you'll be able to channel your value into working on bringing your vision to life. Therefore, you'll guard yourself against those who undervalue you and your work. These people have no place in helping you build your vision other than being a lesson to you. Once you learn that lesson, move along quickly so you don't continue the cycle of allowing the same person to misuse your value repeatedly.

Take ownership of becoming self-aware so that you can move about the world being an asset and knowing when to save valuable time by asking for help and allowing it when needed. As iron sharpens iron, even two dry sticks can create fire. The knowledge of how to use the resources makes the difference between starting a forest fire and a resourceful controlled burn. What are your intentions with the people you have in your life? Are you building together or just having fun?

You can't achieve your goals if you don't have clarity on where you're going.

Growth Mindset vs. Stagnation

It's no one's fault when one person chooses to stay stagnant in life and another chooses to grow to where she wants to be. The problem comes when those who are satisfied with stagnation burden others to stay there with them. We should each enjoy the autonomy of wanting the life we want and working to get it without being burdened with the expectation to accept unintentional living and a world where we can't build the life we choose.

You must know and decide where you're going in life and follow the path that's best for you to get there, hence your milestones and roadmap. This needs to be clearly defined so that you can communicate your vision to others and be consistently aware of the choices you make that either fulfill the vision or push it further away from your grasp.

Sharing your vision and goals with others allows them to serve you as you can serve them. Those conversations must happen to determine if you're both going in the same direction in life, and if not, *how* can the two of you forge a friendship or relationship? Will you be able to serve each other in different areas of your life?

"Surround yourself
with people that
challenge how you
think,
not people that nod
their head and act like
they agree."

—NF

Take inventory of your life, including the people you surround yourself with. Are the people around you assets or liabilities? People who are assets encourage your growth, hold you accountable for your actions and your vision, help you learn more, and possibly even invest in you financially. These people add value to your life in one or more areas for your mental, emotional, spiritual, educational, social, or physical well-being and help you build your future. The people in our lives who are assets love to see us flourish and grow. By adding value to our lives, they get a sense of fulfillment, are carrying out their own life purpose, or could be following the path that God has for them. Just as some people can be assets in our lives, we should strive to be an asset in the lives of others. You won't always be able to be the asset in a friendship dynamic or any other relationship, but that doesn't mean you have to be a liability for someone. There's room for some imbalance in this cycle since the ways you give to each other won't be the same because you'll each have different needs.

Look out for when the people you most often surround yourself with always need you and aren't able, willing, or around to return the favor when you need help. These people are liabilities, and with them, you take on the burden of carrying the entire relationship or friendship. This can also be true for those around you who can't seem to pull their weight. These people become liabilities in your life, costing you time, money, opportunities, and ultimately, the possibility of not meeting your intended goals.

Allowing this behavior can delay your milestones as you carry out your life's purpose or the vision you have for yourself. One person constantly needing the other and never reciprocating is an unfair exchange.

You could be a liability in someone else's life, too. Can you think of any relationship dynamics where you're the one constantly asking for help, favors, a leg up, advice, or money? Those are just a few examples, and just as you don't want people around who only ask those things of you, make sure *you* aren't that person. If you find through self-assessment that you are that person, you've already taken a step to become a better person by reading this book. The next step is to apply this knowledge by *doing* the work.

Now, back to taking inventory. Do you have one or more people in your own life who always ask you for these things with the expectation that you will readily provide for them? If your answer is yes and those same individuals have never or seldom done the same for you nor volunteered to repay you, it's time for you to move on.

Being an asset in others' lives means we're giving of ourselves in a way that helps to build another person by providing wisely used value, building toward their vision or goals.

Sometimes, your "helping" another person means wasting your value because you're giving to a person using you as a crutch instead of making the most of your value. Giving out of the kindness of our hearts is a different ministry than taking on liabilities in the form of people. We can't give freely to bless others nor be an asset to them when we're constantly draining ourselves and not being poured into or refilled. This happens when we take on the liability of others who don't take responsibility for themselves and mislabel it as "helping."

There is a line between giving because you chose to be a blessing and being taken advantage of because you always say yes. Sometimes, this line isn't clear for us to see, understand, or enforce. I can say that, for me, it was a learned skill. I didn't like it, but it was necessary for my growth and advancement. Self-assessing and taking inventory of your friend circle are crucial in ensuring that you're keeping company with people who are assets. The attitudes and behaviors of those around you can be a building block or a stumbling block in how you achieve your vision. Remember, if you hang with five fools, you're bound to be the sixth.

Giving away all your building resources to other people can leave you at a deficit that no one else can fill when you lack people in your circle who are also giving in your life. We're responsible for being wise stewards over our resources, including our energy and time. We aren't supposed to waste what we have by simply throwing it away or giving it away because someone asked for it. This is like taking our resources and just scattering them to the wind with the expectation that we'll always get them back.

There must be a balance to being an asset and being surrounded by people who are assets to your life and vision. Like-minded people should spend more time with one another. Working together is far more powerful than operating as a lone ranger once you choose to let go of people who are liabilities. The issue is when the individuals we surround ourselves with aren't like-minded and are looking for how much they can get from us.

These people are takers.

Takers will continue to take anything you have to offer and then some until you decide they're no longer allowed to take from you. We all know someone audacious enough to ask for more than what you're willing to give or can give. For some personality types, this can become an abusive dynamic because it leaves the Giver at such a deficit that they're no longer able to pursue their dreams and goals. Some Givers even lose things in life to ensure that the Taker can live comfortably. In these situations, the Taker I'm describing is able-bodied and simply refuses to do the work to obtain whatever they're asking the Giver for.

There is a stark difference between a friend or person who needs assistance and someone who wants an easy route by begging her way through life. One person is putting in the work and requests help to go further faster, making good use of people's resources. The opposite is true of the person who has made a habit or even a lifestyle out of asking others for things they won't work to obtain for themselves.

Identifying these people in your life becomes easier because they have no intentions or plans to exert the effort needed to provide these things for themselves. They won't improve their situation in any way other than asking for favors from others. If you're asking yourself, *Am I one of those people?* then chances are you are. But that's okay.

Self-assessment is the first and most important step in this journey, and we'll revisit it in each chapter of this book.

<u>**Chapter 1 Go Notes:**</u>

- Making your vision a reality involves creating a timeline with milestones to measure your progress on your roadmap.

- Your vision requires a measurement tool to ensure that you are, in fact, getting there.

- Consider these questions as you reflect on your current relationships and how you're progressing towards your vision:

  o Are you confident because you've already pruned your social network?
  o Are you currently bearing dead-weight relationships and have been lucky enough to progress in your plans so far?
  o Have you taken the time to consider your needs, wants, and vision and whether some people need to go?
  o Are you holding on to relationships that are parasitic and draining you, but you've grown used to it?

<u>**Chapter 1 Action Exercise**</u>

In your copy of the *Write the Vision Make it Plain: an Everybody Can't Go Journal*, **start writing out your vision, getting as specific about your future as possible**. Create measurable milestones and deadlines along the way so that you can track your progress.

If you need help, follow me on Instagram @everybodycantgoconvospod and DM me, and I'll be glad to help you.

2

SEASON OF GIVING & SEASON OF GRINDING: SOWING AND HARVESTING

Sometimes, we're well-equipped to enter into a giving season, and we can pour freely into others without worrying about how much we have to pour. Our cup runs over into the saucer, fills the saucer to the brim, and spills over onto the table, pooling wide on that tabletop until it eventually reaches the edge and runs onto the floor in a puddle. When our cup is this full, it's easy to pour into others, to share what we have with them, to give to those around us, to impart wisdom, and to invest in, care for, and celebrate with our friends and family. We may ignore how much we're giving for the joy of finally having *something* to share. Are you overpouring in your excitement of the abundance?

Here's the hard truth. Overpouring is not good stewardship of what we've been blessed with and worked hard for. We enter this season after some sowing, planting, tending, and harvesting. When we're not good stewards of our current flow and give away too much to the wrong people and places, we can easily miss the who, how much, and under what circumstances.

By making a habit of this, we can end up paying a price far greater than just doing someone a favor. This isn't for money only! We have to be diligent in properly stewarding our time, energy, emotions, physical space, and connections to other people who are valuable resources. When we're not aware of our vision or don't truly assess our current state, it's easier to get caught in a space of celebration with everyone surrounding us, whether they belong in our space or not. It can feel uncomfortable to celebrate in "invite only" or "closed" spaces when you're used to taking everyone with you for the ride. With today's social media trends, everyone wants to celebrate out loud for the world to see and with many people surrounding them as a part of a status symbol to make the declaration, "We all won together!"

But did you *all* win, and did you win it *together*? Who actually put in work before the celebration?

Don't wait until your winning season and celebration to take inventory of who shows up for you because this isn't an accurate description of who will grind with you.

If your giving season only coincides with your winning season because you have some abundance to share, then you need to make some adjustments. Firstly, your giving shouldn't be predicated only upon whether you have extra to give away. When the other person is deserving, we should be more inclined to make a sacrifice when we're *able*. We mustn't sacrifice for people who won't do the same for us.

That's an adjustment you'll make for yourself, not to edit other people's behavior—especially if you find yourself getting lost in the celebration and giving without a second thought. It's easy to forget during the wins that self-assessment and taking inventory still have their place. We think there's no need for it. I mean, we're celebrating, right!? Because we're winning. There's plenty to go around...right?

Sometimes, the answer is no.

Taking inventory of your most frequent company and those in your outer circle is hard, but it must be done. Why? Because you need to be honest with yourself. We often want to win with the same people we started our journey with, regardless of whether they fit into the picture or not. Part of winning together is *working* together. Why should the people around you benefit from you doing all the work— on your personal development, relationship building, business plans, learning to operate in your gifts, career growth, and the tangible things that come as a byproduct of working on yourself? The scale becomes lopsided if you continue to grow in one or more areas and those around you stay stagnant in the same place. The real problems come when these people want you to stay where they are instead of growing into the place, space, and person you desire to be.

When you wrote down your vision and prayed on it, you set a plan in motion in your life, one that requires work. It's unfair for you not to accomplish your goals and fulfill your vision because someone else feels bad about themselves when they see your vision coming to fruition. Some call it "haters," envy, or jealousy; however those feelings are labeled, it doesn't change the facts. There are many reasons why their vision hasn't happened, and you can't take responsibility for that. It's not your place. Even when others are working on their vision, it may not be their time yet. It's okay to celebrate and be comfortable during a winning season, but don't use that to become undisciplined or lax in who you allow into your circle.

In addition to the winning season and the overflow that comes with it, there is also a grinding season. Your giving season was produced from the seeds you've sown, watered over time, tilled, and grown to the harvest you're gathering. Thinking back to taking inventory of those surrounding you in your winning season, are they the same faces who were present during your season of sowing, when the hard work was happening?

Often during our winning season, a lot of people show up for the party to celebrate the harvest and enjoy the fun, but those same hands weren't there for the planting, watering, or work. Most likely these people won't be there once the season of grinding has returned to maintain such winning seasons. Notice those who show up when you're winning and in a giving season versus where they are when it's time to work. You may need to adjust how much access they have to you.

In our responsibility as good stewards, we need to be mindful of any asset that we can provide in anyone else's life, any value that we can share. We usually think of giving as monetary value, and while cash has its place, there are many ways to give to others. You can give value by:

a) Lending an ear and advice

b) Share your knowledge, information, or resources that help solve a problem

c) Connect people who make good use of their expertise

d) Create social experiences that no one else can, or take on a physical task that another person can't finish

There are many ways to bring value outside of money.

Your family and friends get to benefit from your giving. How much you give to them depends on their relational or physical closeness to you. Each of us has wisdom to impart to someone else who's on a path we've already traveled, even if they're looking for a different outcome or are on a different timeline than we are. The gems we can put into others' hands have value because they help to build some area of their life and could even be a part of their life's vision. How amazing is it that we're helping others achieve their life vision and fulfill their purpose?

With such an important task, we need to own our value and put the proper proverbial price tag on it. It's easier to understand the value of what we have to give when we compare it to currency and give it a "dollar value." While our wisdom has no monetary value, we're often unable to measure that value unless we monetize our wisdom by offering coaching or counseling services. When equipped, we can give advice, share information, or have a conversation that may realign or change someone else's life trajectory. These times are as important for you as for them—not necessarily so that you can lean on them in the future, but so that you're carrying out a part of your own vision and life's purpose by putting some good into the world that you expect to get back in an ever-flowing cycle. This is a part of making relationships reciprocal, in other words, beneficial to both of you.

Accepting Help

Accepting help when the right people offer it during our grinding season is part of properly stewarding our resources and blessings. Because this is the season of sowing and planting, we're not supposed to journey alone. This is where we can get confused, allowing the wrong people to help us plant our garden and stay around to "help" tend it. Having the wrong people around can lead to learning life lessons the hard way. Sometimes, we don't pay close enough attention to who we have around us because we're so used to certain people being there. Our friends and family circle often have familiar faces that aren't helping to plant and tend but are simply present as we're doing all the work ourselves.

We've talked about being good stewards of our time, monitoring who is allowed in our space and who we give to freely, because while we're busy working, it's easy to lose sight of those in our immediate circle. We may become hyper-focused or have tunnel vision on achieving the next goal and neglect to assess those around us. The problem with tunnel vision is focusing only on the goal. We're not looking to the left and right. Without taking the time to pay attention, we aren't sure that the people beside us are working with us as well. Without assessing our relationships, we miss identifying those who are just tagging along as we do all the hard work, and they reap the benefits of simply being in proximity. Who is around you and who is down for you are two different categories of people in your life. It's not right that those who haven't worked with you or alongside you, nor had your best interest at heart, can reap the benefits of your harvest during your winning season. When people show up for your wins, ask yourself: *Were they helpful during my time of hardship and building?*

While some incorrect individuals are "helping" us during the grinding season, there are also the right people who can help us build our vision. They're willing to give to us just as we're willing to give to them. We shouldn't be bound by fear or past pain from the mistake of allowing the wrong people to help us. If this has happened to you with the wrong person(s) coming into your life and tearing down as you were building, causing you to be stuck in the same place, take the experience as a lesson. You know what to recognize sooner and can stop a person in his tracks before the same narrative happens again. You can operate with newfound caution to make a wiser decision the next time (because there will be another time).

I encourage you to embrace and learn to use this caution wisely so that you don't overdo it and reject everyone who comes along. If you're compelled to be overly cautious of every new person who crosses your path, then it's time for another honest self-assessment. You're either in the wrong places physically, are operating in a way that is attracting only negative people, or need to heal from past hurt so that you can discern who's coming to help for a season or a good reason.

In cautiously choosing who we allow in our lives to help us, we must ensure we don't go from one extreme to another. There is a safe and healthy space in the middle. Learn the center of neutrality in allowing and accepting the right help during your grinding season. There will be people who come along your path sent to help you achieve your goals and build out your vision while giving you the opportunity to do the same for others.

These right people may not always look like the circle, group, or crowd you're used to. You may hardly even recognize the person you need the most to help achieve your goal or build your vision because they're so different than who you expected. We tend to spend a lot of time around those who are most like us or those who are most complimentary. This isn't always the path to achieving our goals and vision. We sometimes need those who are opposite us and able to bring a different set of skills to the table that we don't possess. Just because you can do it doesn't mean you should or that you're the best fit for the task. We may know of some of the skills these people naturally possess or may even have a little experience with them, but it's hard for us to execute in these areas on our own, especially when it's against our natural personality.

For the past century, psychologists have agreed that there are essentially four basic personality types. So far, the only one who has naturally and fully operated in all four styles is God. As humans, we lean dominantly into one of the four styles more than the other three and sometimes have two dominating sets of qualities. But that still leaves two qualities that we may be low in and unable to operate in as comfortably or efficiently.

Without this knowledge of the four personality types, the characteristics of the categories, and real-life application of how to work with the strengths, we go into both relationships and business partially equipped with the people skills we need. When we go in blindly, we easily miss our blind spots, which require someone else who's not like us or doesn't follow the same thought patterns. By nature, humans are communal creatures, and we seek out those with the same thought patterns and personality styles as ourselves because, ultimately, it is what we see as the "correct way" of doing things. Without examining ourselves and our behavior style, we won't know our natural strengths and blind spots that someone else can cover. I believe that this assessment is the best way to accept help during your grinding season from those best equipped to help you.

It's also up to us to pray for wisdom to discern the hearts of those naturally equipped to help us in the areas where we're lacking. Lastly, don't forget to pray for yourself to ensure you're not holding people beyond their reason or season in your life, and you in theirs.

My Own Story: Navigating Changing Dynamics

As we moved into adulthood after undergrad with our shiny new degrees, going out into the world to seek out entry-level positions and make the $50,000 salary dream, we still supported one another since our graduation dates were staggered over a few years. I was more than pleased to attend graduation ceremonies for friends before and after my own. We celebrated together because each group of us would be leaving campus for the last time.

Sophia moved into the work world, Liam followed his college sweetheart to Phoenix, Olivia planned to return to New York, and Harper to Cleveland. I missed the missions and laughter with them all as everyone continued their own paths. I missed Harper's powerful yet gentle way of giving advice smoothly while making sure we left feeling empowered if there was anything that had us down. In Sophia's absence, I had to find my own way in theater and learn to speak out alone since I was now the "token" in the program. The big brother's advice that I had over my shoulder since my freshman orientation was gone to Arizona, and I had to learn to watch out for "the guys up to no good." We were all one call away, but things were different during this new grinding season because we were supporting each other in new and different ways.

Amelia, Emma, and I grew closer because we all became Resident Advisors and spent a lot more time together training and working. In our last two years of college, we met and mentored new students with whom we formed bonds. We met Evelyn, who became close with Charlotte, and Nora and Birtha soon followed, becoming part of the friend group after we all graduated.

Amelia, Emma, and I graduated in the following years. We continued to support each other over the summer with our courses and did plenty of partying every weekend. We each brought different strengths and resources to the table. They helped me to look for job leads and get my resume out there because I was preparing for the work world and taking graduate courses in the evenings. I had a car, Emma had parents who funded her lifestyle, and Amelia always provided a helping hand with homework, leads, and bargain hunting. Between the three of us, we were always able to get groceries, have meals together, get gas, and attend off-campus activities together. It was a time of giving and receiving. Collaboration and companionship created some great times and made our day-to-day lives easier.

Graduation always seemed like the time for harvest and celebration because so much work and effort went into earning a degree. We all faced financial challenges, academic rigor, and social and spiritual growth during the experience of earning our bachelor's degrees. During those college summers, we celebrated each other each May, followed by summer birthdays and time off. We had the kind of fun that makes once-in-a-lifetime memories, which soon faded into new relationships and adulting.

I grew from being the one left behind to leaving others behind. My newer friendships changed as I moved into the work world, just like my older friendships changed when they graduated in the years before me. I could get advice from those who had moved on before me and could help and advise those who moved after me.

Truly Helping or Ignorantly Playing God?

When I say we've been ignorant, I mean the literal definition: lacking knowledge, information, or awareness about a particular thing. At one time or another, we've all been guilty of it: playing God and stepping in to "help a friend" or family member when it was time for her to go through her own go-through—in a place where she hit rock bottom, and it was only between God and herself to figure it out.

Many times throughout the Bible, we see His most prolific characters were out alone, and in that isolation, they spent time with God to hear Him speak directly to them, give them directions for how to carry out their purpose, and be a blessing to others, even nations. Adam was alone and given an assignment before God made Eve. Joseph was sold, betrayed, and imprisoned, but saved an entire nation, including the family that betrayed him. Moses was socially isolated but spent time with God and wrote the Torah. Elijah was socially isolated for protection. John (the Beloved) was exiled to an island and wrote the book of Revelation. Paul wrote letters to multiple cities during his isolation in prison, which later became New Testament books, and even Jesus had to spend time in the Garden of Gethsemane alone.

I once heard a sermon that convicted me in this matter. It addressed how we think so highly of ourselves that we inadvertently play God in our own ignorance. This could be because we want all the kudos for helping someone out of a tough spot or because "we'd want someone else to do the same thing for us if we were in trouble..." But we never stop to think that we would never end up in that type of trouble! Are we helping because we're vain, are we helping out of guilt, or are we attempting to do God's work?

After stepping in to save a "friend" or family member too many times, I learned that I was, in fact, robbing them of the opportunity to take accountability and sit with God. I was in their way of learning and preparing to achieve their own vision. There are situations that we were never meant to intervene in, but with our free will and unconscious emotions, we believe we're helping when we're actually prolonging someone else's healing.

I remember in one instance, I got a phone call in the middle of the night, and I should have taken a cue from the dark and stormy weather outside when the call came. Charlotte had called to tell me that Evelyn had been put out of her parents' house for going back to her abusive boyfriend for the third time. Her parents had spotted him driving the car they'd paid the note and insurance for on her behalf. As her friends, we'd had multiple conversations with her about how the relationship wasn't healthy, it was dangerous, and it wasn't a good thing to continuously take back a person who was mentally, emotionally, and physically abusive. Unbeknownst to us, the arguments, stalking, and beating continued, and for whatever reason, she wouldn't let him go.

Her mother, Mrs. Avery, had had enough. She began to pack all of Evelyn's things and just set them outside the home after she saw them. Mrs. Avery was stern-faced, and Mr. Avery cried as he helped his wife to bring all of Evelyn's items outside. As we gathered her things outside, getting soaked in the rain, Mrs. Avery pointed at all of us back and forth saying her final wise words to her daughter and us all: "If he's worth it to you to disrespect your parents, your family, your friends and most importantly, your God, then let him take care of you, since you've abandoned all of the blessings that God had for your life."

Of course, being young, immature, and friends, we felt sorry for her. We even went against Candace's husband, Paul, when he said that the Binns' had been fair and it wasn't our place to intervene. We just couldn't leave our friend and all of her earthly possessions outside in the rain, trying to figure out where to go and what to do.

I received the phone call to do something because I had a large apartment and a spare second bedroom for guests to stay in. Because I had the room, Candace called me to take Evelyn in. Being the helpful soul that I am, I said yes and jumped into action with the rest of our friends to retrieve my friend and her belongings before there was too much additional damage done. After hours of moving all of her things from outside in my small car, a couple of other friends' vehicles, and Candace's husband's pickup truck, we unloaded all of her belongings into the spare bedroom of my second-floor apartment. At the end of everything, I asked her, "...has this been enough? Will you leave him alone? We're trying to help, but you're losing everything..." To that, she looked me directly in the eye, rolled her eyes, grabbed her phone and purse, and headed out the door.

Well, anyone with rational thinking would think that she just needed time to clear her head; that after such an ordeal, she would take time to herself to think about rationalizing what had become of her life so quickly from a string of poor decisions. But that wasn't what happened. She got right back into the same vehicle that her parents paid for and went right back to the very person who caused her livelihood to be pulled right out from under her.

I didn't realize until years later when I heard that sermon about us playing the hero and getting in the way of God's plans for others that that's what I'd done with Evelyn. And when that happens—when we get in the way of God's plans for others and the lesson that He has to grow them through—that same lesson is presented to our friends or family members repeatedly.

Have you ever stopped to think how you may be hindering someone else's life lessons and blessings? After I heard the sermon detailing the places where I had intervened—places where God never meant me to—I definitely felt convicted. I started examining situations where I perhaps should have walked away, but, thank God for Olivia. He used those situations to teach *me* a lesson where a lesson was meant for others. I was inexperienced and didn't know there was such a thing as stepping in the way. I only meant to help.

Once I gained additional knowledge and felt the conviction of the Holy Spirit concerning my oblivious nature, I knew I had to create a hard boundary for myself. I had to learn when to walk away and let someone be alone with God as I had the chance to do at some of my worst moments. There was no one there to save me, no one there to lessen the burden, no one to keep me from learning the life lesson that was set up for me. I had my chance to talk with God, to hear from Him, to let him know how angry I was, how hurt I was, and to ask, "What are you going to do? Can I fix this for me or are You going to fix this situation? What must I do to gain that blessing?"

I was afforded the opportunity to wrestle with God myself, even though that may not be the wisest decision because, of course, we'll never win, but I was angry with Him. I expressed my anger to Him and wrestled with Him anyway, and with my honesty and transparency, I found peace and rest in Him. I grew from situations that some have never gotten up from because there has always been someone to reach out their hand and save them in the physical realm, so spiritually, they were never able to dig deep, heal, and gain clarity for direction in what they were meant to do with their life.

"Nothing grows in comfort. Sacrifice for the sake of your vision."

Takers

We all know people who are always down to receive but not give. That one friend who always forgets his wallet or has to go home early when it's his turn to buy the next round of drinks. The cousin who always needs to borrow money or "hold something" until the next payday, then seldomly, if ever, pays you back. The parent who guilts her adult children into "...obeying thy mother and father..." even when it goes against God's word and His blessing for them. The spouse who "just lets her handle it because she'll take care of it." The adult child who takes advantage of his parents' provisions, refusing to find his way in the world, always leaving the bill to Mom and Dad. I could go on. They'll ask if it's not offered and guilt you by begging or manipulating you to get their way. I call these people Takers. They will take, take, take, take, take until you have nothing left to give, and they'll still expect more from you and offer nothing in return.

We're sometimes pulled into these relationship dynamics (familial, platonic, or romantic) by just being ourselves. When you're naturally a generous person, a social butterfly, or show your value openly, you can become a walking target for Takers to approach to see what they can get.

It's not your fault if you have these types of people in your life, but it is your responsibility—to yourself and to your vision—to set healthy boundaries in your interactions with Takers. Creating new boundaries to protect yourself from misuse is a behavior shift that will take thought, time, and practice to get used to. But with dedication, you will learn to make the necessary changes. Some of us feel a bit of guilt telling someone else "no" so we can say "yes" to ourselves in the short term and "yes" to another step in fulfilling our vision. We'll need to address the feelings we experience in protecting ourselves and our peace as we review our vision and the milestones we set.

We mustn't subject ourselves to a Taker's emotional manipulation. We need to set boundaries to protect ourselves from other people's guilt trips. Their negative talk can impact us in ways that are detrimental to our vision and our mental, emotional, and physical health. By giving in to Takers' demands, we can also leave ourselves at a financial deficit, which would also harm our overall well-being.

Practicing confidently saying no to Takers is easier when we're clear on our vision and keep referring back to it. Remember, your vision has your roadmap and your why written out so that you see what's at stake or what you're delaying when you say yes when you don't want or need to.

When we allow these types of people to attach to us, it's called a **parasitic relationship**. You serve as the host and the other person is a parasite, sucking and draining the life out of you to survive. This draining can come in multiple forms and take different lengths of time to become unbearable for you. People can drain your money, time, or energy.

Parasitic relationships don't always have to be with a Taker who is intentionally living off of us. We must diligently assess relationships that gradually become parasitic as the other person becomes more dependent and the dynamic moves away from reciprocity.

"When someone shows you who they are, believe them, the first time."

—Maya Angelou

Establishing the Infinite Loop

Be proactive in choosing the path that leads to where you want to go. Being reactive instead of proactive wastes other people's time and yours. Time is your most valuable asset and once it is gone you will never get it back. That is why it is of the utmost important to gain control of your time and not squander another second of it on parasitic relationships or Takers. When you only spend your time with other Givers you are able to establish an infinite loop or both giving and receiving.

You cannot create this infinite loop by trying to include people or relationships with those people when they are not giving as well as receiving. There is a disruption in the cycle when there is one or more people siphoning off all (or most) of the energy for themselves. Having people like that involved in the infinite loop of reciprocity, defeat the purpose and destroy the cycle of giving *and* receiving. Assessing the behaviors, actions and motives of those you choose to spend your time with determine whether or not you have the opportunity to create and maintain that infinite loop. Experiencing reciprocity in relationships makes for healthier dynamics, keeping you from the burnout of being overused and under replenished.

When you find yourself in relationship with people who don't complete their part of the infinite loop, your part of the loop is damaged too because the loop is left open. Your precious time and energy is being wasted. Be sure to set boundaries to protect your value and exit when needed.

"You have to be goalin'
together to be lifin'
together."

—Stephanie Jessica
Holley

<u>**Chapter 2 Go Notes:**</u>

- Part of winning together is *working* together.

- There are situations in which we're never meant to intervene, but with our free will and unconscious emotions, we believe we're helping when we're prolonging someone else's healing. Don't play God.

- We all know Takers—people who are always down to receive but not give. It's not your fault if you have Takers in your life, but it is your responsibility—to yourself and your vision—to set healthy boundaries in your interactions with them.

- In a parasitic relationship, you serve as the host and the other person is a parasite, sucking and draining the life out of you to survive. This draining can come in multiple forms and take different lengths of time to become unbearable for you. People can drain your money, time, or energy.

- Be proactive in choosing the path that leads to where you want to go. Being reactive instead of proactive wastes other people's time and yours.

<u>**Chapter 2 Action Exercise**</u>

Think about the Takers in your life. In your journal, write their names and detail what they take from you: money, energy, time, resources, emotions, or all the above.

Once you note that, write out the clear boundary you want to set for them. The boundaries may be different for each person based on how close you are to them, how often you communicate with them, and what form of taking they do.

Lastly, set deadlines for implementing those boundaries. Report those deadlines to an accountability partner or group, and take the first step *today*.

3

THE OLD YOU

"Some people don't know they're running out of time with you."

—Dr. Danielle Penson

We were never meant to stay the same our entire lives. We're born as infants, fully dependent on an adult or someone bigger than us to feed, clothe, protect, and shelter us as we grow into the toddler stage and learn to communicate and move on our own. We develop an independent mind and try to do things on our own. Children are born with just two fears: the fear of falling and the fear of loud noises. All other fears are instilled in us by those who raised us or by events that happen throughout our lives.

Although we were created and made in His image, we were also made to keep learning and growing throughout our lifespan. At a certain point, our physical growth stops, plateaus, and over time begins to deteriorate. However, some people think that when your body stops physically growing, your mind should also stop growing and expanding. Though our physical bodies have stopped growing by our early twenties, our minds are meant to continue to grow and mature well into our 40s and beyond if we choose.

As you continue to grow mentally, you'll hear many of those old phrases, "Well, you've changed, you ain't like you used to be," "you actin' brand new," and so on. The truth is when you're doing the self-work—assessing, realigning, holding yourself accountable for where you are in life so you can create an actionable plan for where you'd like to go—all those phrases are true. And that's not a bad thing! What's *not* true is the negative connotation and feelings evoked through other people's body language, tone, and attitude when they express them regarding the person we're growing into or have become.

Though these phrases can cut deeply if we let them, the fact is that you *have* changed. You gained more knowledge, became a stronger person, and if you're not there already, you'll soon see the tangible results in your life from the changes you've made to grow. So yes, you've changed—you've changed for the better. If those close to you bring it up, it means they can see your transformation and the results of your growth.

"You ain't like you used to be." No. You're not supposed to be the way you were when there's potential and room for you to grow. You can't get to your next level without becoming the person the next level requires. Does that mean you should put on a facade and carry on as a character in your own rendition of a movie about your life? No. It means you found ways to keep and grow your positive attributes and worked on your weaknesses. You're learning more things that make you an asset in others' lives.

When you're being helpful instead of misused until it is damaging to you, when you're aspiring for something more, whether it be within yourself, for your family, at work, or within your community, you'll only be able to serve at your current level. Your dreams and aspirations will require more of you, so you can't be who you used to be if you want to achieve something beyond who you were. It's not your job to help others understand who you need to become to achieve the goals you set for yourself. It's only your responsibility to take ownership of and navigate the best way possible to get there.

Sometimes, the best way possible includes lessons and challenges. If the path is free and clear, then you aren't learning along the way, and if you aren't learning along the way, you aren't growing. If you aren't growing, you're remaining stagnant, and for you or anyone who reads this book, stagnant equals average. Do you want to be mediocre?

My Own Story: Shifts & Separation

As we transitioned from school into the workplace, some went directly into entry-level positions, others stayed behind to pursue graduate degrees, and some did both. Some people in our circle, who only hung out with us occasionally before, became tighter-knit and were now more frequently participating. Since adulthood doesn't always work out exactly as we plan, with that perfect picket fence and 2.5 children by the time we're 25 years old, we began having deeper conversations about life and adulting and how it was so different than the American dream promised to each of us.

Post-recession life was interesting as we attempted to use old tactics to handle the issues of a new frontier. With that, what else was there to do but party, party, and party some more like a never-ending college summer? The only difference was that now that we're adults, we have the funds to do so unapologetically as long as our bills are paid. For me, that meant hanging out with multiple circles any time after work hours on any day. My friends at the time would even come to my job to spend my lunch hour with me, bring me Starbucks when I worked super long shifts, or pop up to bring me dinner and chat on my breaks.

Most times, you could find a combination of both the old crew and the new circle hanging out after work. We never missed Taco Tuesday at the same restaurant at 7:00 p.m. every week and shut down the place after many margaritas, $2 tacos, and however many shots of tequila we could bear. Every Thursday, we went to the same suburban bar with $1 beers and shot girls that bring a tray of tubes to our group of "regulars." Every Friday, we went to the same party on the same strip at the same club, and every time the alarm sounded between songs, we drank as many of the same two- and three-dollar drink specials as we could handle during the song that the sale was on. Every Saturday, we would go downtown and party at the biggest club in the city, with multiple rooms and five DJs spinning different types of music. We got to choose the vibe that we were on that night; our attire was always coordinated. The guys always made themselves available to bring drinks for us and drive us home afterward.

The afterparty was always at my place. I had a 1,500 square-foot apartment with two bedrooms and two bathrooms and plenty of room for anyone who ever wanted to stay over. And people were always over. Why not? There was a huge couch with room for four people to sleep, a whole bedroom, and I had a king-size bed with room for two other people as we commonly had sleepovers in the dorm rooms when we stayed up studying too late and simply didn't want to walk back to our own building.

You could call me The Great Gatsby—anytime I threw a party, everyone who was anyone was there. I had a knack for bringing people together. As I said before, the social circles were separate, but I was a common factor in each of them. I could be friends with people from all different walks of life who carried many different personality traits. I could see the good in everyone in their own unique way. And why wouldn't I?

I was drunk with ambition and fueled by rage after a bad breakup and was able to bounce back like never before: a new graduate degree, a new home, my dream car and being able to party like a rockstar and vacation whenever I wanted. Life seemed great at the time. Looking back now, I'd say that I was young, dumb, and reckless. I thought my social circle was solid, with everyone producing enough to fund what we were doing at that time, which wasn't much, even though we seemed like the Detroit version of Jersey Shore or some other reality TV show on social media. Super glamorous, right? There wasn't anything wrong with what we were doing or the way we were living as we'd all (well, most of us) had graduated with at least an undergrad degree and I had earned my Masters, so why didn't I deserve to let loose and continue the celebration with some of the same people who had been there during the grinding season of making this happen?

We occasionally talked about our next big dreams and goals, and the talk was definitely big. I eventually noticed that as we continued to party our weekends away and meet up for social events, there were far more people around for the fun versus those who were around when it was time to build—when it was time to sit down with our laptops and notebooks to pour over business plans and share information on who could help one another with the different aspects of business building. Our circle became very small. Some were only interested in the prospect of being rich or wealthy because of the lifestyle attached to the fantasy. Not all of us were concerned with building wealth to live a fulfilling life comfortable for ourselves and the families we would eventually create.

It seemed that mindsets were shifting, with some choosing to marry for stability instead of admitting they didn't want to work, some deciding they would never leave their parents' house to continue living above their means, and others spending irresponsibly and getting into the kind of trouble they couldn't get out of.

I ended up in two kinds of trouble: one, the financial trouble of mixing the entrepreneurial dreams with the party lifestyle, and two, celebrating a winning season at the same time as a grinding season, which led to extreme burnout. I wouldn't stop, so my body, mind, and soul stopped me. First, I had to take inventory of how I ended up in that space. Then, I needed to find out who was willing to hold me accountable and be there as I learned to hold myself accountable and take healthier control over my life. Some of the people around me were the wrong people, and I didn't know it until it was time to tear down and rebuild *everything*.

Pruning Process

If we're not careful about taking inventory, some people can wedge their way in during that winning season because we're so busy celebrating. Although we may primarily be surrounded by those who were there during the grinding season, each of those people may not have made an equal sacrifice. This means they may have been present but weren't planting seeds that would yield a harvest or helping to build your vision. Unfortunately, I fell into this state of unawareness, confusing people's presence for their help in building my vision.

While we have our heads down working to create a harvest for our future, some people are just hanging around nearby and looking busy, masquerading as an asset to the team during that grinding season. The wrong people attach themselves to you and gain undue benefits as you celebrate your wins by hanging around while you and others work.

You'll eventually decide that you want to plant new seeds to produce a different harvest or to create an increase during your harvesting season. This deviates from your original standard of work and establishes a new norm for you. When your expected outcome increases, you'll need to change how you work during your grinding season. If you want to harvest something different, you'll have to do something different and become some*one* different. This will disrupt your social circle because people around you are used to operating at the previous standard and are used to *you* operating at that standard.

It's fine to be a dreamer and have huge, lofty goals. Your people may even give you verbal support and encouragement as long as you're just talking about those goals. Once you start executing your vision, your behavior will change as you follow through on actionable steps that lead to building your goals. This will cause a shift in the relationships around you, which will continue as you achieve tangible results.

It's okay to elevate and grow yourself, despite others thinking you should stay the same permanently. You have a responsibility to yourself to continue learning and applying the information you learn to your life in a way that produces the tangible results that *you* want.

This is a growth process for you to own. Simply learning information and storing it without applying it isn't true growth, it's just hoarding. Each time you consume information meant to grow or elevate you, you must also find ways to apply that information. It's not just the information but the *application* that transforms your mind, body, finances, spirit, future, family, and social circle. If you aren't applying the information you've learned, there isn't a point in learning it at all. The application isn't only for yourself, but for you to learn through experience and build credibility to help others in the future.

Think of it like learning to drive a car. You have to physically get behind the wheel to properly teach someone else to drive. If you only learned driving skills in the classroom or on the computer but never got behind the wheel, you can only give a tertiary account of driving a vehicle versus teaching from firsthand experience. There are movements and the feeling of inertia that you can only describe once you've driven. You can describe these things on paper, but you paint a more vivid picture when you explain from your learned, applied, and lived experiences.

Though the point of learning isn't always to teach others, you must first apply the information you learn as part of your growth process. We can always learn more throughout life to become wiser as we age. Even with something as simple (or not so simple) as technology, the frontier is ever-changing, and we must learn new technology as it's released. If we don't keep up with technology as it advances, we'll quickly be left behind. Technological advances are improving or replacing many things in our everyday lives. We now have to know how to use tap readers to make payments and use multiple apps on our cell phones to get more done faster, and we've learned as the complexity grew over time. While some refuse to learn new technology as the world progresses, you must be flexible to navigate everyday life.

"Information applied changes situations."

—J. Quest Green

As you grow and evolve into a higher version of yourself, there will always be an "old you" to rebuild. This reference can be used in both positive and negative ways. While others' descriptions of the "old you" may not always be accurate, it's up to you to self-assess and gauge whether or not their opinions have merit. Are you a new and improved person or someone who has regressed or changed for the worse?

As you grow and apply new information, you'll slowly shed the old skin of your past. This won't always be pleasing to those around you for a few reasons. One, you'll constantly remind them of what they can become but choose not to work for. When your very presence becomes a constant reminder of a person's stagnation, her feelings about your progress will rise to the surface, causing friction in the relationship. These feelings can be jealousy, envy, anger, disappointment, disdain, or sadness. If these negative feelings go unaddressed in a relationship, they'll fester like an open wound, susceptible to infection. These negative feelings can start as a slow burn, and something feels off. You can take into consideration the way the other person must feel at the fact that you both started in the same place, but you continuously elevated to higher levels that the other person hasn't. This speaks more about the other person than it does about you. The other person can harbor feelings of abandonment and resentment.

While we can be empathetic about another person's possible feelings about our growth and success, it's not our burden to bear. We can't navigate those feelings for them. The situation can feel especially difficult when the other person doesn't want to meet you halfway to talk about the negative feelings he is feeling in relation to your growth, next level, or success. How many times have you experienced a friend or acquaintance having a candid conversation plainly stating that she's become distant or started making snarky remarks or comments at or about you because she's jealous of your progression and your growth has stirred up feelings of inadequacy in her? I'm willing to bet my bottom dollar this has never happened to you. If it has, the conversation likely happened after multiple incidents and a specific one prompted the conversation so each of you could decide where you stand in the friendship and whether or not you would continue together.

Here's something else to consider: Are you causing someone else to lose out by not sharing wisdom? You have something within you that someone else needs. However, be careful not to cast your pearls at swine. Your time has value, so ensure you're investing it in those who will make the most of it.

It's easy to forget the value of our time. Its intrinsic value increases throughout our lives. Every time you put work into yourself—a conference, a certification or degree program, therapy, gaining knowledge through books, media resources, or applying your new knowledge—you're building the value of your time. The question to ask yourself is, *how much is my time really worth?* Only you can answer this question. Do it truthfully. We're all susceptible to over- or undervaluing ourselves and what we offer in serving others and ourselves.

To shift your mindset, I suggest you start by calculating a true number in your mind for how much an hour of your time costs. The simplest way to calculate a numeric value for your time is by thinking of your hourly pay. Are you a salaried employee? If so, divide your salary by 2,080. This is your "value" per hour. I put "value" in quotes because this is just a placeholder to help wrap your mind around the worth of your time. It's not what your time is truly worth because I believe you're worth so much more than the number you have in mind.

Being efficient with your time looks like this: While starting his LLC,

John didn't know where to start in terms of filing his paperwork, what forms to fill out, or where to send them. In his research, he found a service that would take care of all this for him for $100. At his day job, John earned approximately $45 per hour gross (before taxes, Social Security, benefits, and 401k contributions). For John to research and figure out how to file the paperwork would take about six hours because he has no clue where or how to begin. Those six hours are worth $270 (six hours x $45 per hour). For John, it will be cheaper to pay for the service and get his time back. His paperwork will be done correctly the first time, and the filing will be completed promptly. If John decides to wait since "he can do it himself," there's an additional risk that he may not complete the task correctly the first time, the task may take far more than six hours, and the task he could be working on in his business will have to wait.

Becoming Separated

It's easy to be humble and loyal to a fault because you're ready and willing to learn, grow, and become a better version of yourself, so you believe everyone in your circle can *and will* do the same thing. This isn't always true. While everyone has an opportunity to go, not everyone is interested in going. We must examine our relationship with each person in our lives on a case-by-case basis when conflict arises. Many times, we don't want to toot our own horn or make ourselves seem conceited and self-absorbed.

Even though humility and loyalty are great qualities to have, you must set boundaries so that those qualities don't become your downfall in your relationships. We'll often let small comments, not-so-jokey jokes, cruel actions, or lack of action go unaddressed because we want to maintain our humility when dealing with social dynamics. We want to keep the peace and grow together. By not addressing these things, though, we're taking part in our own disrespect, allowing someone to treat us poorly. It may be hard to recognize this because the culprit is a friend, mate, or relative. Your relationship with a person doesn't give him or her a warrant to treat you poorly because of his or her self-esteem issues. We must be vigilant and guard ourselves against increasingly toxic friendships as jealousy seeps in. This dynamic doesn't always result in some big blow-up where both people yell and scream at each other, cry, and ultimately storm off. Sometimes, the separation occurs as a gradual wedge driven between the two (or group), and communication decreases over time until it's non-existent. Sometimes there is a silent treatment or stonewalling period, and one person shuts the other out. Other times, one person allows the other to walk away without a fight or a productive conversation to repair and restore the relationship to what it once was.

When there's an irreparable breach in a friendship or a relationship due to another person being unable to handle your growth, it's okay to get comfortable with the discomfort of being separated. Remember, it's not all your fault. It may be no one's fault. Separation may be natural. It isn't always bad and is sometimes required for your elevation. Separation can be downright ugly when there's backstabbing, negative talk, arguing, and lies being spread between individuals or in a group. Today, things can escalate to cyberbullying on social media with a gossip blog-style blowout where not only does a separation occur, but everyone in your social circle (both inner and outer) and sometimes even coworkers and family can watch the drama unfold as the friendship or relationship dissolves. The drama's displayed for the world to see and follow along for a daily dose of literal reality TV, except these actors aren't being paid. You're beefing for free. The "I will hurt you more than you hurt me" attitude can easily consume someone and make him spiral out of control, especially when he has an audience.

It's interesting when someone attacks you because he feels hurt, but you have no idea what you've done to make him so angry at you.

Again, we must realize that many negative feelings manifest as anger when it could be feelings of inadequacy, jealousy, envy, self-doubt, or disappointment that the other person is carrying. When you are that constant reminder for a person who is not committed to growth, it can be enraging. If this shift in behavior toward you is something you've experienced, just know you haven't done anything wrong, and it's okay to leave these people behind. You cannot control someone else's feelings! It's not your job or responsibility. Unfortunately, deciding to forgive someone who treated you this way and letting them back into your life is a slippery slope. Be wise in your decision to do so because there is a chance that they are coming back with a spirit of revenge to humble you by their own devices. Many people who don't address the negative feelings that they have about themselves will take matters into their own hands and attempt to make you feel as small as they feel instead of reaching out to you to learn the things you have and how to apply them.

We're not meant to stay in one physical location, at one job, or live a mundane life. That's unfulfilling. Our bodies are made of roughly 75% water. Stagnant water isn't safe for consumption, so why would we be made of something that's meant to move if we weren't also supposed to keep moving? We don't have to rush into everything like a tsunami, but even the calmest stream trickles.

Accepting the fate of doing the things we weren't created to do has become the norm. Our society promotes the good old "American Dream," which is what you're told to want. But what if you want something more, something different? When you want to be something outside of what you're told to be, the people in the environment you come from will often encourage you to get back in line and conform. Conformity isn't always a negative thing, but in this context, when you long to be free and outgrow the small pot you were planted in, the idea of conformity can be stifling and discouraging.

It comes in many forms: being stuck in the same thought patterns, being forced to stay in the same physical location when you want to leave, or only having relationships that don't enrich your life. All these issues are valid and can be changed with a proper vision, a plan, information, application, commitment, and execution.

Now that we've talked about the things you can control and change, let's talk about the things you can't change as you grow into a new version of yourself. Although you're a great being and God has given you great power, you can't change someone else. Only the person can control that. That said, as we become new, improved, and evolved versions of ourselves, we have to accept that others may not accept who we're becoming. The bigger question is, do *you* like who you're becoming? Are you becoming a person God would be pleased with?

We may need to remove the people who can't accept who we're becoming from our lives; or at least distance them until we've reached a point where being in their presence doesn't stifle our own growth. We also don't want to damage them.

Ask yourself a few questions:

- *Am I stagnant in life right now?*
- *If so, is it on purpose?*
- *Am I comfortable where I am?*
- *Do I want to stay where I am, or do I want to make a shift?*

"You need the right environment to grow. Just like you have a blueprint and a plan before you build your house, you have to be prepared for what you're asking for."

Accepting the Upgraded Version of Yourself

Once you've decided to continue elevating to your next level, remember that you're not saying goodbye to the old you, never to return; you're embracing and welcoming a new version of yourself—keeping the best parts and improving the weaknesses. Accepting the new version of yourself includes accepting everything that comes with it: the amazing new adventures, opportunities, spaces, lessons, also acceptance of new people. Unfortunately, it also means accepting the negative opinions from others about the new you. Not everyone dares to become the person required to achieve and fulfill their life's purpose or vision, to take action on dreams and goals. Some people are *afraid* to aspire to becoming who God has designed them to be. With fears that deep and that big, who are you to think that you would be able to change their mind if God isn't enough for them?

Though it may be a bit exciting to move into the new places, rooms, and spaces afforded to you as this new version of yourself, you may find fear and doubt creeping into your mind in the form of imposter syndrome. It's okay. Many of us feel it, and you're definitely not an imposter. Allow yourself to feel those feelings and remember that we are *growing* through things, not *going* through things. This feeling is just another one of those small steps that will give you big gains in achieving your ultimate goals. In these new places, you'll likely move from being a big fish in a small pond to a small fish in a big pond. That feeling takes some getting used to, but it comes with your growth journey. You'll be exposed to new things; learn to participate in these experiences as part of your journey of expanding who you're becoming. Embrace the change as it comes, and while you're not transforming into someone completely unrecognizable, this is part of the process of adjusting who you were and becoming an improved version of yourself, not making up a character to play as you move through life.

Embrace the changes even when you're afraid, and remember this journey takes time. You'll be exposed to new places, spaces, things, and ideas. You'll seek out opportunities that will mentally, emotionally, spiritually, and financially stretch you further than ever before so that you can build more on the strong foundation that you have worked on tirelessly to become successful.

The new things on the horizon for you may not be anything you've ever heard of or previously considered. The shock of so many new things at once is enough to make anyone raise their hands and surrender to return to the safety of their known life instead of traveling into the unknown. The only problem with keeping that old life is that the unknown has the probability of being glorious. When have we ever been afraid of great things?

When you're pushing hard to reach a goal or milestone, you can experience seasons of exponential growth and get a major return on the work you've put in. These pushes to the finish line can be difficult, though, and you have to love yourself a little more. You're healing, learning, and discovering an elevated version of yourself all at the same time. Be gentle with yourself, have Olivia with *you*. Just as you exercise patience and Olivia with others, do the same for yourself. Accelerated growth can happen all at once after a great, consistent effort over a long time period.

Think of Chinese bamboo. Once the seeds are planted, they must be watered and the soil fertilized every day for five years before anything green sprouts from the ground. However, once the sprout breaks through the ground, the shoot grows up to 90 feet in just five weeks. There will be times when you'll experience this exponential growth rapidly after you've worked consistently at a thing for what seems like a long time.

Keep this in mind as you work. As you outgrow your environment and some of the people in it, people will push you away, leave you behind, and, in some cases, become disloyal or act with low integrity. Since the wrong people don't usually hold themselves accountable for their actions, you'll be blamed for your reaction, whether it be aggression, neutrality, or even complete silence. There's a chance you'll be painted as the villain in someone else's story even when you stay silent about the actions against you.

You should also steer clear of those who believe the rumors because they can be just as damaging to your vision and your peace. Remember, their negativity isn't about you. They don't like you because your success is a constant reminder of what *they* had the opportunity to accomplish but chose not to.

This may be painful, but once you've given your best effort to resolve the conflict and are met with hostile opposition, you'll need to pack up and release those relationships. Continuing to hold out, hoping that the other person—or people—will come around, will only be more damaging for you. It's your choice how much and how long the damage will continue while you're on the short end of the stick. If you've tried your best to resolve conflict with a person or group of people without meaningful progress, then staying with them means you're okay with letting them mistreat you while expecting that they'll eventually get enough and start treating you well again. In my experience, this doesn't end well. I've only seen people become emotional punching bags and lose themselves or experience burnout from others' maltreatment.

You have the opportunity to exercise a healthy boundary, say no more, and use your hard-fought energy to overcome the feelings of grief and guilt from the loss of these relationships damaging your mind, heart, and spirit. Though the separation may not be your fault, it doesn't stop the guilt. Let's be clear: The guilt you feel isn't truly because you've become an elevated version of yourself. It comes from thinking that everyone cares as much as you do and would go to the ends of the earth for people the way you try to. It's natural to feel bad when you enforce a boundary and separate yourself from those who treat you poorly or don't fit your team in a way that promotes growth for yourself and your company.

When we let personal connections dictate our feelings on factual situations, we become discombobulated. Our judgment gets clouded. These actions are not only detrimental to our best interest, but possibly even the person or people you need to release. It's up to us to overcome the feeling of grief, examine the reasons for the split from a factual perspective, and compartmentalize our feelings about situations into a separate category. This will make it easier to work through feeling guilty when you have to do the hard thing in the best interest of everyone involved.

It's okay to grieve the loss of the friendship or relationship with another person because there is a specific void they will leave in your life. Part of your grieving process should include examining whether or not that void will be positive or negative. The people we release along the way aren't all bad, but that doesn't mean the bad parts outweigh the good for what they brought to our lives. We aren't keeping score, but unawareness can cause us to turn a blind eye to someone who's been with us for a long period of time but hasn't practiced mutualism in the relationship. We're not looking for equal giving, but equal sacrifice in relationships because everyone brings something different to the table.

Acknowledging this and becoming aware of it makes it easier for us to see and examine when someone isn't bringing anything to the table or they're bringing the bare minimum. Consider that as you're grieving the loss of a relationship or friendship. When examining the relationship dynamics objectively, you may realize that the person wasn't bringing much value at all or that the season in which you were meant to bless her life has long expired, but you misunderstood what your assignment was with her and attempted to keep her far beyond that expiration date.

The Good Samaritan's True Lesson—It's Not What You Think

This reminds me of the parable of the good Samaritan (Luke 10:25-37). We often take two key lessons from this parable: ensure everyone is treated equally and always help others. I see the Samaritan as a wise person who helped someone and then continued on his path to do what he was supposed to do when he was supposed to do it. Once the Samaritan helped the man who was beaten and left at the side of the road, he made sure he was cared for at an inn and promised the owner he would pay for the expenses when he returned and went on his way. He didn't stay there to tend to the beaten man because he had business in Jericho. Had the Samaritan stayed with the man at the inn while he was resting and recovering, he wouldn't have completed his business in Jericho and would've been out of alignment.

We can help people along the way, but we don't need to derail our plans to help them. It's possible to help someone along your path without stopping and staying there with him, but that takes awareness, wisdom, and execution at a level that requires emotional control. Of course, the "feelings" part of our brains would tell us that it's more compassionate to stay and tend to the man who was beaten and continue to change his bandages each day, telling him stories and spending time encouraging him on his road to recovery. There was business at hand in Jericho, probably also a deadline and, more importantly, a purpose. The Samaritan didn't lose sight of the purpose of his trip. He was able to do some good along the way without destroying his mission.

When we stop to help someone else on the side of the proverbial road in life, that doesn't become our purpose. Our purpose is still our purpose. Though we may take a pause or detour to help someone else, we should still look ahead and keep moving toward that purpose just as fervently as before we stopped to help. When pausing to help someone else damages your purpose, it's not your responsibility to stop and clean up her mess. While this may sound harsh, what's even harsher is the judgment we'll face when we account for everything that kept us from accomplishing our purpose because we were so distracted fixing other things and people we were never meant to.

We should apply this parable not only practically but with a touch of wisdom: If you have the means, do what you can to help someone else and then *be on your way*. Don't stay there. Accomplish your mission and follow up later.

This wisdom does a couple of things for us: First, it gives us the chance to be a blessing to others without overstepping a boundary to play or become a god for them. We're meant to show them how God can use people to be a blessing, but not rob them of an opportunity to build a connection with God in their situation. While we want to help people, it's not our place to become a hindrance to their relationship with Him.

I had to acknowledge the places where I overstayed when I was only meant to be there for a season—the times I was meant to help someone in need and continue on my own path toward my purpose. Think about the side things you helped someone else with that became a distraction, derailing you from your vision and purpose. What happened to your vision as a result?

In closing this chapter, pay close attention to those who "miss the old you." Who or what is the old you that they miss so much? Was it a version of you that was more advantageous to them? How?

More importantly, did that version of you serve *you* in accomplishing your milestones or goals?

<u>**Chapter 3 Go Notes:**</u>

- You're not supposed to stay the way you were when there's potential and room for you to grow. You can't get to your next level without becoming the person the next level requires.

- Accelerated growth can happen all at once after a great, consistent effort over a long period of time. Exercise patience and Olivia for yourself as you do with others.

- Here's how to truly apply the good Samaritan parable: If you have the means, do what you can to help someone else, then be on your way. Don't stay there. Accomplish your mission and follow up later.

<u>**Chapter 3 Action Exercise**</u>

In your journal, answer these questions honestly:

- Are you stagnant in life right now? If so, is it on purpose?
- Are you comfortable where you are?
- Do you want to stay where you are, or do you want to make a shift?
- Did the "old you" serve you in accomplishing your milestones or goals?
- If you want to make a shift, write out the next moves you need to make, assign deadlines to them, and share them with an accountability partner or group to hold you to them, and take the first action step *today*.

4

YOUR SOCIAL CIRCLE: WHO DO YOU SURROUND YOURSELF WITH?

*"One night I prayed to God,
I asked could He please
remove the enemies
from my life
And before you know it,
I started losing friends"*

—Meek Mill, "Who
You're Around" (2011)

My Own Story: Isolation Before Elevation

It happened over a half-decade ago, and I still don't know why to this day... Perhaps just another step in getting me here to write this book for you. In the middle of my workday, I received a barrage of very angry text messages in our group chat telling me what a terrible person I was.

For what? I don't know and have yet to find out.

I was completely blindsided by Evelyn's angry outburst but confused about why the conversation wasn't in person if there was such emotion. This was one of the moments that solidified my break from the group of people I spent so much time with, hosted so many times, traveled with, and would do anything for any time they reached out and asked of me.

Some probably realized the friendship was ending. I was fully immersed in working double shifts six days a week as well as working feverishly on my doctorate. I slept for about three hours a night and took a two-hour nap once I got home after my day, but all anyone noticed at the time was that I was missing in action. I didn't party anymore, made no calls, didn't go out or plan any parties because I was drowning in all the things I felt I needed to do to grow beyond my current circumstances.

My life was meant to be more than working 12-16 hours a day at a job I hated. I was breaking even with the amount of money I spent partying and traveling to cope with how much I hated that job. I decided I would do what I needed to so I could build the foundation to do what I wanted to—not just that weekend, but in *life*.

Others may have been going through their go-through during that time, but the very people who were upset with me never reached out to check on how I was doing when I wasn't the one doing the checking. I was stretched beyond my capacity and was focused on building the foundation for my future. I knew I had to grow, and for whatever reason, my so-called friends were mad about it. They *knew* what my plan was, but I guess no one believed that I was going to do something about it. I had to say yes to myself more, which meant saying no to others in the places where I was previously taken advantage of.

I was blamed for ruining Emma's bachelorette party because I refused to pay $3,000 to foot the bill for two or three other girls a couple of days before the trip. I had to say yes to myself.

Nora was upset that I didn't allow her back to my home after I saw her grope a guy I was dating while she thought I was in the bathroom. A few people told me this, but I'd never actually seen her do it. When multiple people who don't know each other tell me the same thing, is it really a rumor, or is it me foolishly wanting to only see the good in people?

Evelyn reached out to me with the concern that I had been outgrowing our relationship for years and that eventually I would fade away from her and not be available to pick her up out of the rain yet again when she continued her life path. With this backdrop, her text attack a few months later was ironic to me.

This text thread turned into a two-plus-year smear campaign that went all around the city, from people I went to middle school and high school with all the way through our college associates. There were people I hadn't spoken to in years who reached out to me to make sure everything was okay and there was no animosity between us. I started to piece things together once I received a few such phone calls from old friends or acquaintances.

There are always acquaintances you just don't talk to or communicate with often, but when you see them, there's no smoke or animosity. It's just a nice catch-up session to see how everyone's doing in life, and you hug and part ways. These were the ones reaching out with a phone call to make sure all was well because of how the situation went for me as a full-grown adult. It gave me a powerful lesson, and my heart went out to the high school students I taught at the time.

We often talk about how social media isn't real life. It's not important, and we should operate in facts over feelings. However, I quickly discovered how vicious cyberbullying and social media can be and the ways it can impact your life offline even when you're not engaged in it. As an adult, I couldn't imagine the virtual assault on myself and one of my very best friends simply because she chose to stay with me instead of siding with the mutiny against me. I put myself in my students' mind frame and age (14-18 years old) and simply shook my head at the vicious behavior and negative things spewed toward me—someone who'd done nothing to the people who used to be my friends.

It gave me a whole new appreciation for how much we must protect our youth in the digital age. The things they said were merely a nuisance for me because it wasn't true. I'm glad I grew up to be the person I was at the time, because had this barrage of bullying and hate come at me as a teen, it would've been devastating for me.

The cyberbullying and rumors spreading on the internet annoyed me because I knew the people spreading them would never approach me face-to-face to have the conversation, and believe me I tried—both from a place of care and from a place of fists—but I had no success with having the needed conversations to find out where the animosity and anger stemmed from in the first place and what I could do to help.

I now realize that I took on more responsibility than I should have, but at the time, I grieved the loss of those so-called friends. It led me to wrestle with God. We already had a relationship, so why would He take all the people I spent the most time with away from me? They can grow too, right? Wait...*right!*?? Why would He use these people to try to break up my best friend and me? Why would He allow for people who I've done so much for to return the favor void?

I prayed about the situation, and one evening, I angrily asked God, "Why do you want me to be alone?" I heard God's voice so clearly that I didn't have to question it. After everyone was gone, I'd finally gotten my answer. God said to me, "But you're not alone. Look at who's left. What do they have in common?"

It was a thought-provoking answer. I found much peace and continued to move forward, even though what was before me was uncertain. I wasn't alone, I was just isolated for a while.

Amelia and Dominique were the two close friends left, but I'd become distracted and lost focus. Though we never hung out as a trio, they shared a growth mindset. I'd met both at the very beginning of my journey, and the three of us all had a vision, purpose, and very specific goals we worked toward. Even though our education, career, business, and relationship goals weren't intertwined, we nonetheless had specific goals that we discussed with each other and advised each other on. I both gave and received advice from these women and these relationships were *mutual.*

After I examined the facts of my relationships and set aside the feelings of hurt, guilt, and grief, I saw that I hadn't lost any friends at all, and I wasn't alone. The people in my life who masqueraded as friends but weren't mutually beneficial were swept out. I was the one who was constantly giving and constantly losing. Once I came to that hard, very tough realization, I was able to move forward with closing the chapter without closure because the reasons for my maltreatment weren't needed for me to be free. I realized that no matter why I was treated this way, I'd overstayed in a place I should have left and I gave more help than I was meant to give. It was time for me to help *me* and I said yes.

"….I told you the money train's coming and you missed it, I even tried to spin the block back around to come and get you, but you wanted more from me…."

— Meek Mill

Know When to Go

Jealousy and envy for your success or accomplishments can drive a wedge between you and those closest to you. These people could be your social circle, close friends, a romantic partner, or even your family. There will be shifts in how you do things in life and who you do them with. You may be removed from tables where you once sat as protection from once gracious hosts who now serve you poison. This is a natural progression. It's no one's fault when the separation starts. It's just a part of the process, even though it doesn't feel good. It's the same as working out and not feeling good while you're lifting weights. You have to push through those final few reps because your muscles are being torn apart so they can grow back stronger. You don't like the feeling, but the results are well worth it.

In the same way, you'll need to tear down the social structure you knew so you can build a stronger one. It's important to examine who you surround yourself with because you'll become the average of those people.

As you begin to outgrow those around you, you'll find that your different conversations, emerging interests, and dedication to values and principles may no longer align with the company you used to keep. As your mindset shifts, you grow and expand and tend to have less in common with some of the people you once spent most of your time with.

Even though it's an old cliche, do look at and write down the five people you communicate with most often. Then, write down five more names for a total of 10 people.

I'm not expecting that you talk to the same 10 people daily, but if you look at both your primary and secondary circle of influence, you'll spot some similarities between the individuals on that list.

When you examine whether each person is an asset or a liability, you can weigh the pros and cons of keeping them around. This isn't to say that if someone on your list is a complete liability, you should just drop them like a hot coal, but you have the responsibility to yourself and your achievements to modify the time, energy, and resources you put into that relationship.

Gauge whether the relationship is draining you. Gauge the time you spend with them. Are you producing when you're with them? You may need to spend less time with that person and repurpose that time into activities that propel you forward. For example, you may need to reduce your phone time and spend it on your computer doing a course or reading a book to learn more about a new skill, building your business, or even something to help you complete your degree or certification. There will be time for fun later, but time management is important.

You must prioritize those things that will help you grow, move further faster, and achieve your goals. Make time for fun and socializing in your schedule; however, consider the time ratio for additional work on yourself, your business, and your education. It's imperative that we measure the time we're using to build our dream life outside of 'normal business hours'. You may be spending much more time than some of your counterparts who work 40 to 50 hours per week and spend the rest of their time leisurely doing whatever they want to. Your time allotment for socializing won't be the same since you work an additional 10-50 hours toward your vision.

With the milestones and goals you've laid out, you don't have the luxury of leisure for 120-plus hours a week—not when a week only has 168 hours. You have to do the things others won't do so you can have the life others don't have and won't get.

Are You a Mentor or Mentee?

When reviewing the average of the five to 10 people you spend the most time with, look at whether you're bringing the group average up or down. When I did this exercise myself and took a moment of self-reflection, I realized that in my old circle, I brought the average up a lot. I poured into other people, but I had no one above me to pour into me, so I ended up being at the top of the pack. Because of that, I couldn't move past the glass ceiling while I was pulling everyone else up.

I wrongly thought I didn't want to be a taker and that I'd moved beyond being a mentee to someone at a higher level than I was. I thought I had the tools and resources to learn and do all my growing on my own. I was afraid to be frowned upon for asking for help. I was afraid to be a burden to someone else. I was afraid of wasting someone else's resources and letting them down if I failed or fell short of his or her expectations for my success. I didn't realize that I inadvertently decided to go for all of this without support...by being with the wrong people. I spent time pouring into others all the while judging myself for needing help from people who were not in my proximity.

I had to learn through deep introspection that we're never too old or too far along to have someone who knows more than we do give us a helping hand. We're never too old to be a mentee. Again, we're not focused on equal giving, but equal sacrifice, and there are ways you can repay a mentor without doing exactly what the mentor did to pour into you.

We must apply that same concept to our five to 10 people because we should be right in the middle of that pack. There should be some people you can pour into and some who can help, teach, and guide you as you continue to grow. If you're consistently at the top of that list, then who is pouring into you and helping you grow?

Everyone has their own five to 10, and this circle will evolve as we do, sometimes downsizing and other times expanding as life goes on. We must ensure that we take inventory and accept quality people into our lives and vice versa. It's our responsibility to be a quality friend, family member, romantic partner, business partner, or spouse.

Prioritize your plan. When people intentionally or negligently block it, you're responsible for making a change. Allowing others to derail your vision, dreams, and mission can cause you stress and burnout because you're taking on someone else as a burden or priority.

Old keys don't open new doors, and after realizing I hadn't been practicing mutualism with those I spent the most time with, it was time for me to let go of the relationships that didn't serve me well. The distance between us grew wider until it became a strain on us to keep the connection with love.

Facts vs. Feelings

The time came for me to look at my relationships and friendships objectively. I had to cast my feelings aside and repeat to myself: "facts over feelings." The fact was I'd overstayed my welcome with friends who weren't aligned with my vision and had no interest in helping me get there. I'd allowed people to stay close to me for the benefit of being my friend when they were only meant to be there for a reason or season. I ignored the comments of my circle telling me that my vision and I were "too much." I tried to turn temporary relationships into lifelong friendships that weren't meant to be. I had to take responsibility for all the warning signs and red flags I let slide over the years that dissolved the friendships that no longer served me. I had to take responsibility for letting these friendships stay in place for so long that they drained me.

I was so focused on helping others that I didn't realize when to stop and help myself because I felt guilty. I didn't want to be seen as mean, disloyal, a taker, or a betrayer, and I allowed those feelings to become insecurities and get the best of me. I ended up allowing others to treat me with the very behaviors I feared.

After many things came to a chaotic crossroads, I decided to be truthful with myself and knew it was time to let go. I didn't continue to reach out to repair friendships or relationships meant to be left as they were in the past. I decided to stop hurting myself by allowing others to hurt me, using me for their benefit while I always received less from them. The friendships weren't all bad, but they had a specific purpose in my life at specific times.

I was responsible for not paying attention to small grievances that grew into larger and deeper problems we didn't address. I unconsciously knew that had I brought up the issue(s) for discussion and resolution, I'd be met with immaturity and aggression, so I avoided crucial conversations that would have let me know, one way or another, whether a person was there for the friendship or not.

I also had to take responsibility for keeping people around long after I should've let go because I lived without boundaries for myself, which left me open for additional incidents until I was forced to part ways. I was building with one hand and being torn down with the other by keeping company with the wrong people. I made that choice and was responsible for changing the narrative.

We must put on our oxygen masks first when the plane is going down.

Grieving Lost Relationships

Forgiveness doesn't require you to let people back into your life in the same position or with the same level of access they previously had. While it's important to forgive and even forget the wrongs done against us, no scripture instructs us to allow a wolf back into the safety of our sheep pen.

A part of letting go is examining facts and being objective, but there is also time for feelings. Friendship breakups are real, and there are feelings involved that you'll need to work through to become a better person.

When mourning lost friendships and relationships, we must remember to forgive the other person and ourselves. We must forgive ourselves for allowing others to waste our most valuable commodity: time. We must also forgive ourselves for holding onto people who weren't holding onto us and even those who were holding onto us but became parasitic.

The element of forgiveness is crucial to the process because it allows us to work through our feelings and get to the facts so we can use them objectively for the best outcomes. If we just bury our feelings and don't address them, we'll end up harboring the grief and guilt that comes with the loss. It may even cause us to be blind to the fact that these relationships were no longer serving us or even moved into a season of becoming draining to both us and our purpose. When this happens, we're not using our resources wisely, which means we're being poor stewards. This isn't what God wants for us.

Whether we're aware of it or not, we bear the responsibility for how we use what we have. Oftentimes we think that being good stewards of our resources only applies to money, but it also includes our time. Allowing others to waste it, especially once we know they're wasting it, becomes an "us" problem, not a "them" problem.

It takes time to overcome the loss and sadness that come with elevating to the next level and accepting that everybody can't go with you. Though we want to see the best in those around us, what they could become, their gifts and talents, and how they could use them to propel themselves forward to a greater purpose, it's not our job to make others do that.

When we choose to do that for ourselves, the changes we experience can cause us to feel guilty because we're only focusing on the best in others. That narrow focus actively ignores two very important things: free will and desire. Not everyone desires to work and grow to their fullest potential, though everyone wants the result and may even feel entitled to your hard work.

Who's willing to admit that they aren't willing to work for the things they claim to want out of life? Even if people admit they're comfortable right where they are, they won't exactly say, "I'm okay with being complacent where I am right now..." They'll say, "I'm doing fine here for now," and still talk about what they want to accomplish or attain in the future but do nothing about it.

It's not our job to harbor guilt for those who have untapped potential that we can see would propel them forward to the things they desire. You'll need to find a way to release that feeling because you can't make anyone do anything. You can't control anybody else's behavior. You can only try your best to be a positive influence and help where the person needs you to, and even that has limitations. You can't build a person's life and do everything for her.

This is true of children, too. You provide your kids with everything they need during infancy, toddlerhood, adolescence, and young adulthood. However, even with the human beings you brought into the world, you can only "do it for them" for so long. Children learn and become autonomous over time.

Being a wise resource to others means you're not wasting your time and energy with people who haven't and won't get started, but instead focusing on people who have a clear vision with milestones and have communicated how you can help them achieve it. Do you see the difference? One person has already *started* the work, and he has a space for you to pour into him and be a helping hand to an already existing vision. The other has not established anything about her vision. You may have an idea of a vision for her and that's not your place. When you domutually that, you begin to take ownership and become invested in a vision that doesn't belong to you *or* her; it's something you made up *for* her.

When we look at a situation this way, we can conclude that a large part of our guilt in leaving others is our own doing. We feel guilty that we've left behind a person and a made-up vision. We have to stop setting expectations for others that they haven't expressed or even accepted. When we view others through the lens of their untapped potential, we create a belief system about them that's contrary to who they've shown us they are. We can't hold them accountable for the vision we created for them in our own head nor can we hold them responsible for our guilt when it's time for us to part ways.

Each person has the right to choose the type of life that he or she wants to live. We have to make sure we don't overstep boundaries with anything beyond being an encourager in the person's life until that season ends, and we must ensure we don't stay beyond that. Just as others are entitled to live in their untapped potential, we're entitled to move on and continue to grow.

From Feelings to Facts

After we've processed our feelings of grief and guilt from the loss of a non-mutual relationship, we can move into examining the facts more easily. At this point, we view things objectively, make effective decisions on how we allot our time for mutually beneficial relationships, and recreate or adjust healthy boundaries surrounding the relationships we need in our next phase. You need the right people to fit in the right positions, just like you need the right tool for the right job.

When you're taking inventory of the five to 10 people you spend the most time with and realize you need to make adjustments, you can take a direct approach by having a conversation to find out if someone will come along for the journey or not. This won't always work out in your favor and isn't the only approach. Another option is simply adjusting yourself and your schedule and explaining the adjustments if you're asked why. It's up to you whether you communicate aloud before or during this transition, or you can simply make the necessary changes.

The same goes for employees in your business. Though they may have been there with you for the launch of your startup, if they haven't grown as the company grows and learned along the way as you have, you may need to reassess their role in it. Some people may feel a sense of entitlement because they've been there since the business's humble beginnings, but they shouldn't be allowed that liberty. As your business grows, you may need to give an old employee different tasks. Sometimes, there's an upskilling opportunity to train old employees to step into new roles as the company grows, and they can learn to fit the new mold based on new needs that present themselves. If those two scenarios aren't met within your company, then it's time to consider letting people go. If your business's workload or needs aren't being met once it's scaled to a certain size, you'll start to see a profit loss or hit a plateau based on your employees' performance. Once you've presented everyone with the opportunity to continue growing with the business, and they refuse that opportunity, you no longer need to force the issue. Creating a disciplinary step program complete with training and redirection should be a last resort after providing others the opportunity to upskill and grow with your business.

Making the necessary adjustments with friends is a cakewalk compared to making the needed adjustments with family. In an upcoming chapter, we'll explore the family dynamics that can work against you when you're not equipped with the proper boundaries and knowledge.

Forgiveness

Forgiveness isn't just having Olivia for the other person. Most importantly, it's for you. You won't move past those feelings of guilt and grief and move forward in a healthy and positive way without it. Forgiveness comes with the acceptance that the relationship has run its course, and what was once a beautiful friendship may no longer serve either of you because you're now going in different directions. It may be impossible for the two of you or the group to continue to move forward positively as long as you all stay together. We often don't consider how we may be hindering each other's growth and forward movement by staying in proximity to others who aren't a part of our current season. Not all separations have to be final—it's up to you to adjust where you need to. The separation may be temporary because you're building and doing things you haven't done regularly before so that you can live the life that you haven't lived before.

Forgiveness comes with many things for you: freedom, clarity, and a clear conscience. It builds the foundation for moving forward in the direction you're meant to move in. Since you're grieving some lost relationships, there's no purpose in you hurting for free. I'm not a fan of going through painful situations only to be on a merry-go-round right back to that painful situation when I have the knowledge and power to stop it from occurring again. When you allow circumstances or people to hurt you continuously and you do nothing to stop it once you're aware, I call that "hurting for free."

With any emotional pain, there's a learning opportunity to become stronger and more knowledgeable in an area of our lives. But that only happens if we self-assess to find out what gaps we have, fill those gaps, and focus on a solution. Your pain has a cost or value, and you determine that value because you're the one who must turn it into something profitable so you can learn from the situation.

People will badmouth you. They'll talk negatively about you when they lose access to you, which means they see you as an asset. No one is upset about losing someone who was a liability in their life and brought nothing of value to the table. This is a large part of the negativity and confusion that comes with severing draining friendships and relationships that aren't serving you properly, meaning the dynamic isn't mutually beneficial. I'll remind you again: not equal giving, but equal sacrifice.

When you're going through that painful transition and having hurtful things said or spread about you, a lesson is one of the most valuable returns you can get. You'll learn to work through your grief, ask yourself the questions to get over feeling guilty for moving on, and forgive for your sake, not just for the other person's.

In return for your pain, you'll get a clear conscience and a path forward without being weighed down by someone who wants to be carried, would slow down your journey, or possibly even be detrimental to your entire operation.

Take time to revisit your inventory. Look at your vision and what your life is meant to accomplish while you're here. If the people in your inventory aren't aligned with your vision and purpose, then you have some hard decisions and honest assessments to make.

You must keep a facts-over-feelings mindset to make accurate assessments. That way, you can be a good steward of your time, money, energy, and assistance and ultimately make your vision reality.

Reclaiming Your Time

Remember that your most important resource is your time. While we hear the most often about being good stewards of our money, money is ever flowing. Energy can be replenished with the proper rest, relaxation, and time to clear your mental and emotional space. But time is the one resource that, once expended, you'll never get back. You won't be able to make it up or regain what was lost in that area of life.

There's always a time for fun, work, planning, and harvesting. There's also a time to move forward, separate, rise above, and get away from the people who distract you from achieving your goals. That last one is the most crucial yet the most ignored when we lose focus on building our vision.

As you inventory, create space, and change who you spend the most time with to create the life you've always wanted, you'll gain another opportunity, not a task. You get the opportunity to rebuild. You can rebuild everything in your life, from how you spend your time to who you spend it with, and how you spend that time once you're together. You may find that when rebuilding and examining your daily structure you'll have more time alone. Take information and execute.

Another thing you'll notice when you're intentional is you have much more time to spend with God and to find peace and rest. When you seek to grow stronger in your spiritual walk and go farther than you've ever gone before in life, cultivating a relationship with God is just as important and necessary as cultivating your earthly friendships and relationships.

Realizing we can't help everyone and take them with us is sometimes heartbreaking because we feel a strong need to help others when they won't (notice I didn't say *can't*) help themselves. It's easy to ignore the facts of someone else's life choices when we're always providing. We get used to it. In other words, we get used to being used and the person gets used to begging because he knows we'll give without opposition or resistance. This can become such a norm that we aren't bothered by the constant requests for assistance in things he can do for himself because we become numb to it and it becomes a part of our routine.

There's a difference between helping and taking care of another adult's responsibilities simply because you're willing and he's asking. The beneficiary won't always take it well when you finally have the conversation to change this behavior. You've become a resource to him, and you're effectively cutting off or reducing his access to that resource, so he'll feel you're stripping him of something valuable. The fact is, you are!

However, it's unfair that your value is expended on another fully capable individual when you can put that time and energy elsewhere to grow. This doesn't make you a bad person for changing the level of access another individual has to you so that you can do something more to elevate yourself. When you've identified that you don't like the person's constant taking, there's no good reason for the person to demand access to you. That's reason enough for you to restrict or eliminate that access.

Deciding to protect yourself, your vision, and your feelings (in a healthy way) isn't something to feel guilty about. I know this is easier said than done, but you don't deserve to be taken advantage of, whether you're comfortable with your current position in life or you want to grow further. Push through those feelings of guilt and pray for clarity and understanding as you work through the negative feelings and sometimes ill-treatment that come with advocating for yourself.

While you may end up in isolation and grieving the loss of relationships, you'll become strong enough to stand on what's best for you and, ultimately, what other involved parties need to move forward as well. Think of it like this: If you were providing a true need that the other person can't live without, then he'll figure out how to get it done. If he chooses to go without it once you stop providing, then that means he didn't need it in the first place.

When you try out this boundary, you'll find that many things "only you can do" for the person will magically be fulfilled by someone else. When I implemented this boundary to protect my peace and my mental and emotional health, I was met with opposition, but I also found great relief when other people completed the tasks I was doing. I regained some of my valuable time needed elsewhere on things to grow and *recharge* me in between my daily grind.

Regaining your time to rest and recharge is highly important and often overlooked, not only by us but by those who ask us to take on another task. Others are often oblivious to how full our schedules are, so it's up to us to be sure we're protecting our time by not overbooking ourselves.

Isolation is Only a Season

We weren't created to be alone. Don't confuse a season of separation to grow, mend, or build for a new way of life in which you're permanently alone and unable to depend on others when you need help. Just as we can't fully commit ourselves to being solely dependent on others, we're also not made to be alone to fend for ourselves in all things. It takes a team and support network to accomplish anything, but the key is identifying the *right* team to get you there. Your time of separation and isolation should be used wisely to self-assess and reflect on your choices in people to examine *how* you got there. This is your time to adjust your acceptance of others and your level of giving to them, create healthy boundaries for yourself, and heal from the guilt and grieving that comes with letting some people go in your pursuit of achieving your vision.

Everyone wasn't meant to be there and partake in the blessings and fruits of your labor. They may even cause you to work in vain—you may be stagnant because of the company you've kept. Once the "dead weight" is released, then you're free to fly higher. When loneliness strikes, stay positive and make the absolute best of this time because it won't last forever, and there is great value in working on yourself while you're clear of your previous distractions. Also, don't forget to have a talk with God about it. More than once.

There are conversations we have with ourselves and with God. God is all-seeing, all-knowing, omnipotent, and omnipresent. Those qualities are all plural. So, why would God expect us to live a singular and solitary life? It only took a few days before He decided it wasn't good for Adam to be alone. Adam seemed to be doing fine by himself, but God knows what's best for us. If He's everywhere all the time, why would we think He won't use others to help and guide us? God speaks and works in all ways all the time.

The same goes for those seasonal relationships that we have to release—God uses those dynamics to work in our lives, too. He uses those interactions to lead us to something better, and we have free will to decide whether or not to embrace the journey to something better. It's part of our free will to choose wisely who we allow in the different seasons of our lives and how they can be involved. We can choose whether the relationship will positively or negatively impact us when the season ends. We learn lessons as we move through life and sometimes the same situation occurs, repeating the same dynamics with different people until we get it right.

Grow Yourself, Grow Your Value

Your growth isn't only for you. Those who are connected to you will benefit from your growth as well. That alone holds value and responsibility. Your growth in any area takes energy, effort, resources, and, most importantly, time. When you decide to invest in yourself, whether through formal education, mastermind groups, YouTube University, courses, workshops, or prayer and Bible study, you commit to learning things beyond yourself and ultimately become a better person. You become more knowledgeable, having progressed and applied the new knowledge to change your situation, yourself, and your business.

Your market value increases in business, social, and spiritual settings when you do the work to apply the new things you've learned to your life. You can measure how much more valuable you can become to others, and remember, these people should be reciprocal relationships. Once you know your value, you're responsible for using your time, words, learning, money, and spirit far more carefully. Your circle can waste your new earned value, or it can multiply it. What others do with your value is up to you based on your healthy boundaries, identifying those reciprocal relationships, being aware of equal sacrifice, and considering your role as a mentor or mentee in those relationships.

Have you ever found that when you're on your soapbox with another person, you sometimes talk to yourself, too? That's me all the time!

Being a person of value and surrounded by people of value will cause you to grow exponentially. People of value reflect what you're putting into the world and don't leave you drained once you've spent time together. When people in your life are removed or escorted out, leave the vacancy there. The void they left is healing for a better reason. Whoever you're letting go, ask yourself: *Will this person contribute to where I want to be one year from now?*

"Stop crying over people who left you when times were hard because you weren't going to win with them anyway…So consider it a blessing that they aren't in your presence."

—Carlas "CJ" Quinney, Jr.

<u>**Chapter 4 Go Notes:**</u>

- You can't control anybody else's behavior. You can only try your best to be a positive influence and help where the person needs you to, and even that has limitations.

- When mourning lost friendships and relationships, you have to forgive the other person and yourself.

- Forgiveness isn't just having Olivia for the other person. Most importantly, it's for you. You won't move past those feelings of guilt and grief without it.

- When you decide to invest in yourself, you commit to learning things beyond yourself and ultimately become a better person.

- Being a person of value and surrounded by people of value will cause you to grow exponentially.

<u>**Chapter 4 Action Exercises**</u>

1. In your journal, take inventory of the top 10 people you most frequently communicate with. Next to each name, note if the person is an asset to you or a liability. Also, do the opposite: note if you are an asset or a liability for that person. This will make the decision to keep them or leave them much easier for you.

2. Set aside time this week to hear from God about His purpose for your life. Ask Him about your top 10 people list in the exercise above. Whatever you believe He tells you to do, write those instructions in your journal, give yourself a deadline for each task (or ask Him for those deadlines), and complete them.

Writing Out Your Vision & Roadmap Just Got Easier.

Get your copy of the companion book, *Write the Vision, Make it Plain: an Everybody Can't Go Journal*, **today**.

Carve out your vision and make life-changing breakthroughs in the journal as you work through this book.

Available now on Amazon.com: https://a.co/d/4CgDFKL

5

MAKING SPACE: ESTABLISHING NEW RELATIONSHIPS

You have to make space for new things, new people, new experiences, new opportunities, and new exposure.

To gain something, you must lose something. Losing something or *someone(s)* can feel devastating at first, but that absence is needed to clear the way for something or someone better. We usually only hear this language surrounding a romantic breakup, but it's the same for friendship breakups, exiting a social circle, leaving a job, or separating from any type of draining relationship (family, etc.). The void that's left in your life after a relationship ends has a purpose if you allow that purpose to be served.

The void provides room for you to grow, to prepare yourself and that space for someone else to fill later. The difference is that person will be higher quality and have better character, moving in a new season or for a new reason. You may even be blessed enough to have someone who will move into that space for a lifetime. But for the right people to come and fill that space and not become just another lesson for you, you must prepare yourself and that space. There is greater responsibility in growth and elevation.

Establishing new relationships isn't always easy, especially after we've worked through our feelings of guilt and grieving the loss of the relationships we needed to remove from our lives. Allow yourself to go through your full grieving process to ensure that you come out on the other side with clarity on why you needed to let go and have closure on moving on. You'll be better able to apply your learned tools, techniques, skills, and a more valuable mindset surrounding the relationships that you cultivate in your life moving forward. That way, your life doesn't become a revolving door for the same type of people in different bodies.

How many times have we met someone who has the same friend, just in the form of many different people? Or dates the same person in a different body? Or even complains about the same repeated poor behavior from a singular person but he or she allows that behavior to show up repeatedly in multiple forms?

Sometimes, we can't notice a person's patterns while she is there, but only in the peace you gain from her absence. You don't realize that you're better off without some people in your life until you have the space to navigate without them. As with anything else, we must prepare ourselves mentally, spiritually, and emotionally to properly accept new people into our lives who bring us equal value.

It can be scary to trust someone new coming into our circle or connecting with us. On the surface, it's always easy to make new acquaintances because of the cultural expectation of being "polite," but the connections I'm speaking of go beyond the surface level politeness, hand shaking, exchanging light conversation, or even enjoying a meal together. Establishing new relationships requires a level of trust that allows a person to truly get to know who you are, what your values are, the principles you live by, and even delving as deep as to share information about your life's vision with him or her. Now, that's some serious stuff, and we don't share those things with everyone we know, because not everyone in our proximity deserves to know the innermost workings of our lives, minds, and hearts.

Healing is an essential part of building new relationships in a healthy way because if we don't face the negative feelings that previously grieved us, our losses will cause us to be highly skeptical of new people who come into our lives, even if they're meant for mutual benefit or for good. We miss out on the growth that comes with forgiveness and the wisdom to move forward.

Not taking the opportunity to heal during the loss leaves us susceptible to letting negative feelings grow like an infection in an open festering wound. Instead of cleaning it, disinfecting and bandaging it so that it can heal properly and without a ragged scar, we ignore it and let dirt and debris further exacerbate the initial injury. The concept of leaving an injury open to germs in the elements sounds irresponsible, irrational, and downright silly, but when we look at this concept in terms of burying our emotions, even after exercising facts over feelings. We can recall times throughout our lives where we've allowed this to happen, and I'm willing to bet you've allowed it to happen more than once, as have I.

Part of the goal as you read through these chapters is to embrace what is hard so that you can have beautiful healing instead of that ragged scar that I referenced above. There's a big difference in the appearance of a wound that's been sterilized, stitched, and bandaged until healed and a wound that was left to mend on its own without any intention or care.

Your life will reflect the same things when you take the time to address the hurt and pain that comes with transitioning out of the relationships that drain you or don't serve you. In the same way that an attended wound can turn into an unnoticeable scar when properly cared for, so can the emotional wounds that come from the very real truth that everybody can't go. The renewed energy that radiates from you as you continue to move throughout your life from a healed space is a large part of preparing for healthier and mutually beneficial relationships.

I promise you, new people are coming, and to be blessed with the mutually beneficial relationships that await you, you'll need to do the additional work of making the space suitable for these new people. I don't mean physical space; I mean in your head and your heart. You'll need to ensure you're in position to accept new people in your life, exercise the wisdom to know who these new people are, and verify that they are the right people to fill those voids. Being in the right place to establish new relationships is a benefit of releasing the wrong people from your life. The people you had to release may have been the company that was keeping you from the new rooms you're entering now because they weren't equipped or qualified to be in those rooms. Even with others recognizing your value, you may have been seen as a liability in new rooms because of the company you kept. This was more than true for me as I transitioned from the void and healing to establishing new relationships.

Everybody can't go where God is taking you, and not everyone who has traveled part of your life's journey with you has been equipped the same as you. In your quest to become separate, whole, set aside, and carry favor, more will be required of you, including elevating the caliber of people you choose to surround yourself with. We aren't meant to elevate alone, but that doesn't mean that everyone who begins the journey with you will finish it with you. You all were likely never headed to the same destination!

Every expressway has exits on both sides every few miles, and many vehicles travel side by side on the same expressway for a while until someone exits to head to their destination. Other cars are taking your same exit, but if you're constantly checking your rearview mirror to look back at the past, then you won't see what's ahead or the other vehicles beside you. If you operate looking back, you'll miss who's taking that exit with you.

There will be people alongside you, but they won't always be the same people you started with. New people will be headed in the same direction, and it's your responsibility to be ready and open to new connections with them. You'll continue to move and grow with new people who want the same things you want. You can only go so far alone, just like you can't continue with the wrong people.

You've done work, made major efforts to become your best self, and continue to work at that version of you each day. That extra effort qualifies you for environments, rooms, and opportunities that the general population isn't offered. You have to work to grow out of average and become above average, good, great, and then phenomenal.

In that case, you can't expect that everyone can gain the same access you've earned if they haven't put in work as well. Or, while others may have done the work in their own way, it also doesn't mean that they're equipped the same way you are. Being equipped for a specific job is also a part of being qualified.

Someone may have been putting in just as much work as you have, but not in the same areas, so you may be qualified for a different environment and opportunities as you both grow in different directions. That doesn't make either of your areas or growth trajectories better than the other, just better suited for each of you.

You can keep company because there will be some overlaps since you're both growing in your own experiences. There will still be some separation, though, because your parallel journeys have two different destinations. This junction may lead both of you into different environments, rooms, or spaces. Even in that situation everybody can't go, but your friendship doesn't have to be left behind. You're both growing and supportive of one another, just with your own respective goals. You may not be meant to go into the next room that's meant for your good friend. That doesn't mean you won't meet back up to celebrate after you've done what you need to in those separate rooms.

"Ask and you shall receive, seek and ye shall find, knock and the door shall be opened unto you."

— Matthew 7:7-8 (KJV)

The next place or room you belong in may not be the destination for everyone you are with. It's yours, so lay hold of it. Don't give away what belongs to you because it *belongs to you.* There's a reason why it is yours and there's work to be done with that blessing. Allowing another person to keep you from stepping into that room is only delaying your growth and giving away what's yours. You can't be upset if the blessing goes to someone else and they do with it what you should've done.

Are you ready to let go? Be afraid, but do it anyway. You can do it scared, or you can freeze in fear. Either way, you're afraid; choose to be afraid, but with results. The absolute worst that can happen is you move afraid and end up gaining a lesson.

Everyone won't be prepared, equipped, welcomed, or allowed on the other side of the door you're meant to walk through. They may not have earned it (not allowed). If you have your ticket to gain entry, you must go alone. You might hesitate to leave for the sake of others you want to wait on or mentor, but waiting could mean that neither of you will gain access because the door closed and the opportunity is lost. The window of opportunity is gone and now you're stuck on the outside, locked away from the blessing(s) you were meant to obtain and the chance to usher others into the blessing as well. Will you take responsibility for the lost opportunity? Have you robbed yourself or others with this action?

Everybody can't go to the end of the vision you were given, built, and worked for. It's your job to let go of the wrong people, whether others are clinging to you, or you're clinging to the past, or won't allow the space for your future. If you continue to hold on, God can and will allow those people to hurt you enough that you *have to* let go. Like a hot pan burning you, the relationship gets hotter the longer you hold it until you can no longer bear the pain. Your brain takes over, and you have to let go. You could've let go as soon as you touched the pan and minimized the damage.

Letting go and creating space sometimes allows the opportunity to repair the bond in the future when the time is right. The choice to keep holding on can continue to cause damage until the pain is beyond repair. Relationships with severe and tragic endings are partially our responsibility because, with wisdom, we can give the relationship room to breathe and possibly dissolve it a bit more peacefully if the season has ended. Accepting the coming end of a season with someone makes the healing process a bit easier because we don't continuously hold on long enough to be hurt as we let go.

My Story: Letting Go, Grieving & Rebuilding

I asked God to remove enemies from my life, and I thought I could see clearly who meant me no good. I looked around at the things that were coming undone, and I was mad. I wrestled with God until He pointed out to me that I wasn't alone. I didn't realize I was being molded to prepare a space for new relationships in my life—better relationships with mutually beneficial people who also knew what it was like to move from one space to another and shed people whose season had expired in their lives.

I was apprehensive at first because I didn't know what to expect next. I thought my small tribe of three was what I would finish out life with, but God had been preparing me for new connections. I needed to be more than an improved version of me. To receive these new people, I had to BE a new, healthy space to accept growing people who were also *giving* people. It was a major adjustment for me because I didn't realize until I was there that I'd become conditioned to a social circle of takers who rarely gave. I had to learn what mutualism is and how to experience it without fear.

I didn't realize some of the new rooms I'd be welcomed into once I was ready and alone. I was the friend that always said, "everybody can go," "everybody eats," and "you can do anything that I can do." But that's not true. Everybody *can't* go. Everybody couldn't go with me or were even welcome into the same rooms and spaces I was invited into.

The reason why some of my blessings were delayed (but thank God not denied) is that I would've tried to drag baggage into the room with me. By baggage, I mean some of the old friends that I allowed to come with me everywhere I went—even into rooms they were never meant to be in—and it damaged my credibility.

It wasn't until I separated from certain people long-term that I realized all the blessings and opportunities that were presented to me. I was finally in the right position to take advantage of the opportunities and be successful. I had to self-assess and examine the fact that I wouldn't have been ready or prepared to walk into those rooms and spaces without disrupting them as opposed to adding value. My baggage would've caused a negative distraction that would permanently ruin my reputation and cost me future opportunities and blessings. The people in these new spaces had already done a level of self-work and ascended to a level my old friends couldn't serve. By keeping the wrong company, I also wouldn't be invited to the *next* room or space.

It's nothing against me as a person, it's nothing against them as the people they were, it's just that by keeping company with those who chose to stay stagnant at a certain place in life and by my choosing to evolve and ascend to a different level in my own life, the only way for me to move forward was to make the exit for myself and allow those doors to be shut so that new ones could be opened to me.

The new people I keep company with both personally and professionally are people who wouldn't welcome the mindset and actions of those I had to leave behind. I learned that it's okay to leave behind situations that I've outgrown and the people who choose to stay in those situations and seasons in life. It was my responsibility to myself to work through the grieving process of cutting old connections and relationships. By allowing myself to mourn the loss of those connections, I was able to find healing that opened me to new relationships that elevated me to my next level.

I noticed that the people I left behind have one thing in common from the time we all met in undergrad until the present: they hadn't accomplished much more than what we'd done over a decade ago. During those 10 years, I worked, learned, gained more education, and had exposure to many enriching experiences and activities.

That's not to say that everything was perfect and all unicorns and rainbows, because that 10-year span came with some tough times. I experienced moving from place to place, struggling to find my purpose in life, and extreme burnout from working in several companies. In those times, I had to pay close attention to who was around, who had my back, and how. That blanket statement—who's around and who has our back—can cause us to keep people in our lives who should be released. We all know misery loves company, but we don't think of this when we're considering who "has our back" in those times when we need support, love, and wise counsel.

I was surrounded by people who were always down for the ride no matter what I was going through because they had less than me and were looking for a free party. Because I always believed that everyone I spent time with was no different than I was, and because I was so accepting of everyone, their baggage, and their situations, I was blind to their need to leech off of me to be fulfilled. I didn't realize I was the host to parasitic people and relationships. I was blind to the fact that everyone can't accomplish the things that I can and that others around me weren't willing to work at the level that I did to achieve their dreams and goals.

We all started in the same place, and as time went on, I put in the work and others didn't. I started pulling away from the pack, and envy and jealousy set in. I had to learn that humility doesn't mean that everyone is as capable or willing as you.

Rebuilding Trust with New People, Rebuilding Trust Within You

I want you to become comfortable with clearing space and resting in the loneliness that may follow. You can rebuild trust not only by forgiving those you had to leave behind as well as yourself, but you can build trust with new people. This is often easier because you can start on a clean slate and build trust from scratch. It's a must-have skill to prevent getting left behind because you're skeptical of everyone who comes into your life after you've experienced some type of painful relationship break, whether it be romantic, friend, family member, or professional. The pace at which you choose to learn to rebuild trust and exercise it in your life is up to you. I won't say "the sooner the better" because some of us need more time to properly heal so that we aren't going out into the world damaging others due to our mistrust from previous relationships.

To rebuild trust with new people is also to rebuild trust within yourself. You're the common denominator in all these relationships, and while you may not have deserved the way you were treated or misused, you won't be able to go forward without making some additional changes to yourself. We've already walked through forgiving yourself as you continue to pick up the pieces and build into your best self. Once you forgive yourself, you'll need to rebuild trust in yourself. If you can't trust yourself, then who else can you trust? I'll even go so far as to ask this: If you can't trust yourself, are you truly able to trust God with the plan that He has for your life?

As new people come into your life, a level of skepticism is natural. That primal neurological response warning you about letting someone new in may trigger a fight or flight scenario. I can assure you there's no need to stay on high or even medium alert, but instead focus on being aware. Learning new acquaintances' intentions can help you exercise trust in those who can become new friends, business partners, associates, and social circles.

Every relationship doesn't have to be super deep or time-consuming. It's okay to have acquaintances with whom you have a good relationship in an untraditional sense. True friendships are few and far between, and honestly, we don't have the time to dedicate to huge friend groups. But we do have time to spend in community with those whose mindset matches ours and who desire a mutually beneficial relationship. There will always be time for fun, games, and relaxation, and there will also be time for accountability and taking care of business.

As you grow, you'll begin to attract people who have been through the same fire you've traveled through. You'll join a community with people who not only want your value but also recognize and respect it. You'll attract people who are on the same upward trajectory you're on and experience what it feels like to grow with others instead of pulling the dead weight of those who aren't putting forth the same effort as you.

Once you experience these types of people and you're able to keep community with them (and not just be an island surrounded by others), you'll start to embrace a feeling of rest and safety. Though you may still have that rush of adrenaline, feelings of excitement, or even nervousness when walking into a room of new people, you'll experience the joy of getting to know others and paying attention to what they can bring to your life and what you can bring to theirs for a positive dynamic that will bring more great things to the world.

We have to grow through things to get ready for the people we're supposed to do life with. We can't just stay ready for this. With a bit of hardship, we first learn to get ready and *then* stay ready so that we can become the person required to maintain these beneficial relationships. The void left by the wrong people, the ones who can't go, was too small for the new, larger-than-life people who are coming to fill the space. This is why we must keep growing and expanding so that space becomes big enough to hold the new people of greater value who will work by our side in making our dreams a reality. You'll move from being with people who tell you, "You can't do it because it's too much" to being with the people who ask you, "How will you accomplish it? Because anything is possible."

Not only will the new people ask you how, but they'll also believe just as hard as you do, and you'll finally be able to feel what it's like to have a "you" as a friend.

> *"...We headed to the top, if you coming, come on..."*
>
> —Jay-Z

<u>**Chapter 5 Go Notes:**</u>

- Become comfortable with clearing space and resting in the loneliness that may follow.

- Forgiving and rebuilding trust with yourself is important to make room for new and greater connections in your life.

<u>**Chapter 5 Action Exercises**</u>

1) Have you let someone go that weighed you down? Have you fully grieved the loss? If not, seek out a confidant, spiritual counselor, or therapist to talk through it.

2) Do you currently trust yourself? If not, why not? Write your answer in your journal. Then, answer this: What would it take for you to trust yourself going forward?

Whatever you write down as your answer, *start doing it every day.*

6

FAMILY DYNAMICS

efore I begin, if you're someone who has wholeheartedly decided, "Can't nobody tell me nothin' about my [insert family member here]," then just skip this chapter altogether and take advantage of the many other ways you can grow from this book. This subject requires extreme maturity and is one that most people will never overcome due to deeply ingrained issues. Everything you were raised to believe is about to be challenged, completely negated, even. And whether it seems like it or not, this is for a better outcome for everyone involved, though each person won't agree or see it that way. Those avidly against what I propose in this chapter are exactly the family members that will harm your vision the most.

We've all heard "family first" and "blood is thicker than water," but we know things aren't always that simple in real life, and the Bible is often misquoted. Unfortunately, manmade religious ways of glorifying God have led some of us to believe we must endure suffering at the hands and mouths of our family. If no one's ever told you, I'll be the first to say: that is not biblical.

Well, the scripture fragment *is* in the Bible, but people, especially family, have taken that fragment totally out of context. 1 John 5:6 and Matthew 27:34: "...blood is thicker than water..." This text refers to the blood of Christ and has nothing to do with the bond of family. Once I studied the Bible for myself and found out this scripture was misquoted, I couldn't help but wonder about the origins of the misquote. I decided that it came from an overly religious guilt trip, with the scripture used to manipulate and control someone else.

Boundaries are a great way to ensure that family members hold their rightful place in your life while also keeping your peace, building your vision, and maintaining your love for them. It will not only help you, but it will also help your family members interact with you in a healthy way that allows your bond to grow stronger instead of you just tolerating each other. How many of us want to be merely tolerated by others (especially family) when we can be loved and cherished in so many other ways?

With boundaries, we can help our family members, even the ones we avoid the most, learn how to love us in a way we're receptive to. Doing that creates peace in a tumultuous dynamic and reduces or can eliminate drama altogether (when family is dealing with you, anyway).

<u>Disclaimer:</u> Nothing in this chapter is meant to endorse, encourage, teach, or promote tolerance for sexual, physical, mental, or emotional abuse of any kind. If at any time, *anyone*, relative or not, is abusive toward you, you are not required to stay, be subjected to, or accept the behavior quietly.

There are multiple resources to get assistance:

988 Suicide & Crisis Lifeline

Phone: 988

Website: 988lifeline.org

This is a national network providing 24/7, free and confidential support for individuals in distress. They also have an online chat available through the website.

Crisis Text Line - This service offers free, 24/7 support via text messaging.

Text HOME to 741741

The Trevor Project - Provides crisis intervention and suicide prevention services to LGBTQ young people

Phone: 1-866-488-7386

Website: thetrevorproject.org

Veterans Crisis Line - Provides crisis support for veterans and their families

Dial 988, then press 1

Website: veteranscrisisline.net

National Domestic Violence Hotline - Offers 24/7 support for victims of domestic violence

Phone: 1-800-799-7233

Website: thehotline.org

National Sexual Assault Hotline - Provides support for survivors of sexual assault

Phone: 1-800-656-HOPE

Website: rainn.org

Childhelp USA - Provides 24/7 support for child abuse

Phone: 1-800-422-4453

Website: childhelp.org

National Human Trafficking Hotline

Phone: 1-888-373-7888

Website: humantraffickinghotline.org

SAMHSA National Helpline - Offers referrals for substance abuse and mental health treatment

Phone: 1-800-662-HELP (4357)

Website: samhsa.gov/find-help/national-helpline

Of course, in case of immediate danger, always call 911.

While setting fair and safe boundaries takes commitment, patience, and time, there's a chance that setting a boundary and staying in contact with a family member (or several) may still be detrimental to you. You're never required to be in community with anyone who causes you mental harm, financial hardship, or emotional damage, regardless of how much that person loves you and you love them.

One of the hardest things to do in life is take inventory of our family and address ill treatment. This is especially hard when the issue(s) has nothing to do with a death or physical abuse; these are extreme cases in which separating for your peace are choices more accepted by family. But family members can often verbally abuse us, and we're conditioned to believe that words are "just words" and they "can never hurt" us. We've all been on the receiving end of the truth: words *can* and *do* hurt! Both life and death are in the power of the tongue, yet we're more ready to allow those related to us to speak anything over our lives just because they're family.

Speaking love and encouragement into your life is a great blessing, depending on the family you were born into. By contrast, speaking negativity and brokenness can be the very thing that binds you to underachievement and stagnation.

There are two extremes and some less extreme cases in a mostly loving family with issues that arise here and there throughout life. But I caution you to be careful when claiming every family has drama.

We've normalized this saying out of context and if you're unhappy and not achieving, then you probably have more than "a little family drama" going on. The problem is you've just grown accustomed to it. However, that doesn't make it healthy or the best option for you. Small issues can easily snowball into big issues if we don't communicate effectively. This includes openness and sharing our experience as we grow and pursue our vision. Being open gives family members a chance to be a part of our vision and contribute to the life we're building. Usually our vision includes family that will contribute to it. When this isn't the case, though, we have to accept the things we can't change and make adjustments.

Some of the most common issues I've encountered involve family members being pessimistic of visions and goals, family members violating established boundaries (financial, verbal, or physical), and the refusal to accept growth, evolution, and changing dynamics. While there's a myriad of family boundary issues that can apply here, we'll focus on these three overarching themes.

I am willing to bet, even if you're quiet about it, that if you're reading this book, you have high aspirations, dreams, and a plan for getting to your goals. That said, sometimes it's hard to find safe spaces to share your lofty vision and goals. We can always tell God our plans, and He answers in His ways, but never in a way that is discouraging and leaves us a dead end. Only people can give us such a letdown.

Many times, family members can contribute to negative thoughts and self-talk so strongly because we're used to them being there, and we're used to listening to and internalizing their voices. Conversations that include dream-killing phrases can have negative effects on our pursuit of our life's vision:

"You can't do that..."

"How can you think you will ever accomplish that..."

"You're not smart/talented/good looking/well-spoken/liked enough to...."

"You can't even...so, how are you supposed to..."

"You can never make enough money to fund..."

"You want too much..."

"You can't have..."

"Why would you ever even consider..."

While some family may mean well and want to protect you, be of assistance or educate you on the harmful ways of the world, you can choose to continue to allow this type of encouragement—or lack thereof—to be spoken over your life. It's up to us to accept or reprove conversation that goes against our vision and goals.

In every season, just as all your friends or associates can't go, sometimes you must distance yourself from family members (or in-laws) who are detrimental to your vision and dreams. That's not to say you're throwing them away forever, but you can make the choice to communicate less if that family member can't (or won't) stop sowing seeds of doubt into your mind. This can be a difficult bond to modify depending on the person's relation to you, but temporary distance (mentally and or physically) may be the very thing you need to grow your confidence to the level of achieving what you're striving for.

A real-life "some, not all" example is going away to college, the military or trade school. There's a reason why higher learning and post-high school learning experiences involve a fully immersive experience that involves removing many of the things we grew up with and became accustomed to. Circumstances and the environment inevitably force us to grow and require the removal of the familiar (family) to continue a learning experience and transition into adulthood. Even for those who get a later start instead of directly after high school, they'll need to set certain time boundaries, focus on their commitment to completing a specific educational goal, and dedicate themselves to the rigid process. For a successful post-high school experience (or at least passing), there is a period of separation from family, even if it's in increments of one to three hours at a time for class, plus study time.

The school example is the gentlest but necessary boundary setting goal or aspiration for a person to pursue. This same boundary can be applied to purposefully using time and physical space between yourself and family to fulfill a goal or to complete a step in your vision where the familial connection can be a hindrance. The choice doesn't always feel good, but it may be required for your growth.

This is a personal choice that can be made with the family you were born into, but the dynamics change when a family comes *from* you. Don't confuse the two. The responsibility of creating a family is very different from the responsibility you have to the family you were born into. We can't control the family we were born into, but we definitely have choices in how the family that comes from us is built, nurtured, and will live life. We make a series of decisions, starting from the mate we choose or who we allow to choose us, when setting the foundation for the family we will create. We have the option to go backward and make corrections to move forward and build our legacy stronger and wiser than the way we were born and raised.

"...look at the world from a different angle... Don't believe what you believe just 'cause that's how they raised you. Think your own thoughts, don't let them do it for you..."

—NF

To tackle the issues we've discussed so far, we can learn and practice some things that are healthier for us and the vision we're building. We need to distance ourselves from negative talk; this goes for family members, too. Any discouraging conversation can be cut short, and you can change the subject or physically remove yourself from the dynamic. End the phone call or visit to preserve your energy.

Decide on and enforce hard boundaries for parasitic family relationships. Say "no" to the cousin, parent, or adult child who always asks to borrow money but doesn't pay it back. No is a complete sentence. You don't owe any additional explanation for your decision; it is your choice. Your house carries your rules on visitation and access. People don't get to go against your wishes just because they always have or because they're your (insert family relation here).

Finally, don't shy away from modifying access levels while you're pursuing certain goals. There are times when you'll need to separate yourself and keep your head down to work to get to your next level. Don't allow the way you were raised to pull you back down at every step you accomplish. We're striving to build and continue building, not tear down with the other hand. If the hands that are tearing down what you're building belong to family members, then they too must go. The black sheep of the family is often misunderstood, judged, and has a hard time communicating what and who they are as an individual within a collective that has a different ideology and outlook on life. When you're striving for more than the environment you grew up in, it's hard to face the fact that all of your family won't be able to go with you. Some won't want to. The family you create through marriage and possibly having children is the one you're most responsible for.

My Own Story: Learning Outside of the Nest

I found myself using my separation time from family to study and learn things outside of the way I was raised. I was free to learn how to "adult" my way and was able to see that not everything I grew up learning was the only way of the world. I experienced new denominations of Christianity and learned what I agreed or disagreed with without having others tell me that the way other people did things was wrong. I was free to learn about other religions from real people. I was able to be in community with them and ask questions about their religion and answer questions about my own. I was free to hang out with people from other cultures and backgrounds. We had politically incorrect conversations to learn each other's ways.

I learned the differences in what family means, the roles and responsibilities of each family member in different cultures, and what life is like for families whose lineage wasn't affected by chattel slavery but had been touched by war or persecution. We shared the good and the bad, and the questionable without having hovering ears to influence our learning about one another. I learned to create my own informed opinions by learning to consider multiple angles of situations, not just examining with the lens my biological family taught me to have.

It was also easier for me to study in undergrad and grad school when I was away from home. I didn't realize how much more efficient I was at studying and getting my homework done when I was away from familiar distractions. It was easy to study in the familiar and comfortable environment of the home I grew up in, but it was also easy to be interrupted in my thoughts, hear something else going on in the house or for someone to pop in to ask a question. I didn't find out until later that it takes about 23 minutes to get refocused once your concentration is broken.

I found myself leaving the house to study at my local Starbucks, in the corner with my headphones on and caffeine within arm's reach. This was my perfect combo because I wasn't familiar with the people around me, and the shop's noises weren't anything familiar for my ears to perk up to. It was far easier to block out the noise and people because I had no personal connection to them.

Exposure to new experiences gave me greater access to learn what I needed to do to fulfill my big goals that my family deemed unsafe and unstable. My family taught me that working a good job was preferred to entrepreneurship to maintain stability. Go to college, put money in my 401k, and everything would be comfortable and predictable. I know you can chuckle with me at such teachings because, well, the Great Recession all but destroyed that theory, even though it was a good idea for the previous two generations of my family.

I had to take risks and figure some things out on my own to build the life I wanted despite being told it was wrong because "we've always done things this way."

You won't always need to stop communicating with family to heal if you're able to accept the things you can't change, but place boundaries where necessary so you don't have to be hurt. To learn yourself, you sometimes need to take extended time away from the family you grew up in. Why do you think young adults "go away to college" to have an experience of learning to be themselves outside of the nest they were raised in? This learning experience can look different for each person depending on how much independence she needs, the desire to grow beyond what her family thinks she should be, and whether or not she has the freedom and is encouraged to grow beyond the family's beliefs.

Within my own family I had a time of separation because I had to be broken, to unlearn, heal, and gain understanding outside myself and the way I was raised, learn to establish healthy boundaries, refine those boundaries as needed, and stretch in the area of forgiveness in a new way that ultimately built a better me to be able to pour from a full cup.

I shifted my focus to creating the family that would come from me and less on trying to control the circumstances of the one I was born into. I could offer a positive influence, but I couldn't force other people to grow in the ways I had. I had to accept the things I couldn't change. I kept in close contact with some and always made myself available for the younger ones who needed me, but I released any unreciprocated or negative lateral familial ties. I chose to take some time away from those who spoke negatively about my vision, goals, and dreams.

I'd grown frustrated with speeches of how I "couldn't do" this or that, or "resources were too limited." I noticed the forever-angry personality traits that had nothing encouraging to say about my dreams. Family members would rebut any idea or conversation about my life vision with, "...Just go to work, keep your head down, and make a living." Of course, I was disgusted with the thought of giving up after everything I worked, fought, and grew through so far. I still couldn't understand why people in my own family would want so little for me. I figured they would at least listen to my desires and let me share my dreams without dashing them on the rocks every...single...time.

Over time, I learned that they were speaking from their own experience and limitations. I didn't have to accept that for my life, and I have the power to decide for myself what my life will be. As I grew, I learned to drown out their negative voices and opinions and replace them with my own voice. I poured positive thoughts into myself and my vision.

Once I found my true voice, uninfluenced by others' negativity and unapologetically me, I was able to communicate with them in a way that was no longer detrimental to my vision. But that strengthening took separation, building myself with positive resources and unlearning limiting beliefs that had been instilled in me for years.

I can see each family member going through their own journey, and I don't have to take responsibility for trying to fix things for everyone. We can all have separate lives and desires but still come together at the appropriate times. I respected the space for others to make their own journeys so we could come back together with new perspectives to help family members help themselves. My time away allowed me the space to learn ways to help my family from the inside out in ways I wouldn't have been able to if I had stayed close. Though I can offer help, I have no expectations that others will grow, and that's okay for them.

It's hard to unlearn the way you grew up when you're still in the same environment that bred the doubts you have, even when those doubts are against your natural thought pattern and preferences. You may even be so indoctrinated with the things you grew up learning that you don't even know what your inner voice sounds like because you were taught to bury, stifle, or silence it. When this happens, we don't even realize at what point we stopped dreaming and listening to our own inner voice telling us to go for the things we're passionate about because we'll sacrifice those passions for those we love.

What if we were brave enough to fight for the things we're passionate about until we're successful and then take our family by the hand and show them what growth is possible instead of saying, "I told you so...".

Family, like any other people, can also distract you from your vision or hinder your progress. We established earlier that jealousy can breed and grow when you start at the same point as another person, but you end up going farther faster—by work, favor, or blessings.

But we all know a family where you really can't believe that two or three siblings grew up in the same house with the same parents and were taught the same values, because of how one sibling turns out versus another.

Yeah, that's me, too.

Look at the story of Joseph, who was once the youngest and smallest of his brothers, but they felt great jealousy at the favor their father (and ultimately God) had for him. They betrayed him because of it. But during his isolation, he grew through his struggles and became a man with the means to save the same family members (his brothers) that had foolishly betrayed him.

When we're called or chosen, there are scenarios we'll have to deal with as a part of the journey we are meant to take. There will be many people, including some from your own family, that will feel jealous of the favor you receive. To whom much is given, much is required, and having those you were born to love be against you can be a part of what's "required" to become what God has designed you to be. There's no way around it without causing further delay or damage or robbing someone, maybe even yourself, of blessings. The work isn't just for us. It's also for others, and sometimes for the very ones who were against you.

Giving from a place of peace is far easier and more impactful than trying to force yourself by pouring from an empty cup. From a place of peace, you're giving from abundance instead of struggling to give when you barely have anything to give. If you haven't achieved your milestones or goals, then you need to focus on where you're headed. When you get to your promised land, then it's not draining for you because you now have it to give from a full cup.

Is there a person or distraction taking you off course? Are you allowing or enabling this behavior? Who is losing when you allow this distraction to continue? Do you have more to lose by staying there or more to gain by going without them?

Getting past this part of life takes courage, strength, healing, and acceptance. Every family member may not grow and make changes with you. That doesn't mean that family isn't important. It just means that you'll need to adjust how you deal with each family member to maintain your growth and become a leading example of what's possible.

If you stay committed to this difficult process, you'll be surprised how much you'll be able to influence positivity and change the dynamic of your family. If you choose not to take on such a great responsibility, that is perfectly good for you as well. The choice is yours to make, and accepting the things you can't change may be the best option for you.

<u>**Chapter 6 Go Notes:**</u>

- With family members, you must accept the things you can't change. You're not responsible for forcing them to grow with you, and some may even be jealous of your journey.

- You can't choose the family you were born into, but you're responsible for the family that comes from you.

- If your family members have always instilled limiting beliefs in you and cast doubt on your growth, limit their access to you so you can focus and continue to grow.

<u>**Chapter 6 Action Exercises**</u>

1) Take time to think about your family relationships. Is/are there a person(s) or distraction taking you off course?

Are you allowing or enabling this behavior? If yes, who is losing when you allow this distraction to continue?

Do you have more to lose by staying there or more to gain by going without the person(s)?

2) If you need to, research online how to have brave conversations, then schedule time with the family member(s) you're ready to create boundaries for and have the brave conversation. Your life and success depend on it.

7

DATING & MARRIAGE

Romantic relationships have several levels of commitment. There can be a big debate on what the labels are, but for this book I'll speak on dating, an official (mutually agreed) relationship, and marriage. Aside from the labels we put on romantic relationships, it's good to know who we are and what our vision is before we choose who to do life with. Many romantic relationships and marriages end because of one person's growth.

When I researched the top reasons for divorce, I came across a few we don't talk about often enough: lack of communication, constant arguing, unrealistic expectations, and not being prepared for marriage. These specific reasons intrigue me because they can all be solved before divorce court by taking your vision seriously.

We've worked through writing out what your life vision looks like, and if you haven't already, take the time to expand on what your ideal mate looks like. Not physically (though you can list those traits as well), but what are your ideal mate's values? How would you like the person to show up for you? What qualities would you like the person to have? What does your ideal day-to-day life look like? What does your spiritual life together look like? What's the financial structure of your household?

I encourage you to take it a step further and write down your non-negotiables. What are the things that you absolutely can't deal with in a romantic relationship? The "in sickness and in health" vow means different things to different people. What does that mean for you? Would you accept a mate who refuses premarital counseling? Would you consider someone who doesn't want children? What if you found out that the two of you *can't* have children? Are you for or against medical fertility treatment, and how much is too much to spend on conceiving?

Take time to work through your wants, needs, and non-negotiables for a mate so you can have greater success in choosing or accepting a mate who can grow with you.

As a single person, we'll focus on dating to find the "right one," but it's more important to make sure that *you* are the right one before going on the hunt. In your seasons of waiting for the relationship you want, you have to work on yourself. Self-assessment in your romantic relationship or partnership is a key part of building yourself, growing, and achieving your vision because it can make or break your vision. Who you choose to be with romantically as you're growing and executing your vision is even more important than your platonic relationships. This person will become your right hand simply due to proximity. This person's mindset, values, and quality will influence the way you follow your vision roadmap.

Simply put, they'll help or harm the road to your vision.

While it's usually advised to not date potential, there are tangible ways to see the progress of someone who's growing just as you are. The most important choice begins with knowing yourself, your vision, and who fits the criteria to be your right hand as you make your vision happen. It's not just about where you are now. Will the person fit where you're going?

While we can't control the future, we do have *insight* on the type of life we're working toward, and we can use *foresight* to make wiser decisions based upon the values, behaviors, and characteristics of a potential mate. This isn't about judging every potential mate who's not the right one for you, but about being knowledgeable enough about yourself and your vision to tell who isn't fit for the job long term and then acknowledging a reason, season, or lifetime person in dating. When you find that lifetime person and you're ready, that's when marriage happens. (Unless you decide that marriage isn't what you want, that is. These principles can still apply to your life partner. If you'd like to be permanently single, skip to the next chapter.)

Identifying the values, characteristics, and traits of your ideal mate will help you choose a partner who aligns with your vision. When you and your partner aren't aligned, you can both be moving but not in the same direction, not on the same timetable, and not even aiming at the same target.

We discussed moving at the same time but taking a different path to get to the same destination. In romantic relationships, this gets even more complex because you're combining your efforts, and two visions are becoming one. You'll both compromise in some places, and in others, you'll save each other time and combine resources. These are great things to do when you're both headed to the same place. Difficulty arises in misalignment—when you both have different destinations and resentment begins to brew.

Lack of communication can be addressed ahead of time by knowing your vision, including what your ideal partner looks like, how they fit into your vision, and who you need to be to contribute to the romantic relationship you want.

Effectively communicating your vision and your plan to get there minimizes arguments. Effective communication includes managing your emotions during your seasons of isolation, learning to effectively establish boundaries, and being understanding of others' feelings as you continue your growth journey. This doesn't mean that disagreements won't happen, but choosing a partner that you can have the needed conversation with is a must.

You can manage any unrealistic expectations through self-awareness first and using your time of singleness and isolation to learn what you need and want from a mate, as well as what's intolerable for you. You can't cram a potential mate into a box they don't fit in, nor can you make them big enough to fill shoes that they were never going to fit. It's up to you to know when the potential is only potential and no tangible results are showing the potential is being used.

Not being prepared for marriage can be tackled by getting ready, starting with, you guessed it, your vision. Your vision to build with someone can even inform the decisions you make while dating, which prevents the opportunity for the wrong mate to tear you and your vision down.

Sometimes, you don't know what you don't know until you're involved and realize your current partner wasn't meant to be your lifetime partner. This scenario can be very difficult because the relationship dynamic begins to crumble if you really had your heart set on that one person, but consider whether that person was meant or equipped to handle the new you at your next level(s) of greatness.

My Own Story: Trapped with a Bad Choice

I made the mistake of being in a relationship with a man who was fit for my season at that time and wasn't meant to go any further in my journey because his close connection to me would've held me back from flying. I made this mistake twice as an adult, and I realize that in both cases, I hadn't begun with the end in mind. I had some insight into myself but hadn't formulated the full picture. I accepted a mate based only on where I was at the time, without assessing my potential growth and the future fit based upon their vision (or lack thereof). I hadn't yet written my vision, and when I did, it was very clear that they weren't part of it and didn't fit my destination. Each was a fit for a season, so I couldn't stay there with them. I had to choose before it was too late to let go of seasonal people and stop trying to fit them into lifetime positions.

Had I chosen to stay, I would've paid dearly in stifling my growth and hit the proverbial glass ceiling. Before I reached it, I could see the glass above my head, and I fought to push the glass higher, but deep down, I knew it wouldn't move. I had to choose to release the season and start over. I didn't want to be stagnant. I didn't desire only the "look" of success; I truly wanted to be successful. The process and the work to become a success as I'd mapped out in my vision was very different than the mate I accepted.

My mom pointed out to me very early on that the mate I had accepted wasn't fit for where I was headed in life. I was under the false presumption that once I made it far enough in life, he would look at my progress and also grow. I was sadly mistaken and, at the time, didn't know that it wasn't my place to try to grow another person without his commitment to a growth process. I had to grow into some of the new rooms, spaces, and places that I was meant to be in before I was able to understand, a couple of years after the relationship had dissolved, exactly what my mother meant.

This person wasn't prepared to pull his weight in conversation, work ethic, or lifestyle with any of my friends, colleagues, or social circles, despite having a certain "look".

If I had stayed beyond the season or returned to familiarity for fear of the unknown, one of two scenarios would have played out:

1. Two to three years later, I would've been miserable and in a draining relationship where I'd be forced to remain stagnant to avoid the second scenario.
2. I would continue to grow, and my previous partner would've stayed in the same place in life. I would've spent more and more time away from home, away from my relationship or marriage, growing into a person that he would hardly recognize.

My outer appearance would stay the same, if not improve over time, but the inner me and the energy radiating for me would continue to evolve. My accomplishments would be vastly different and run circles around the person who decided to stay in one place. I'm sure that after a while I would've grown resentful of not having enough support or the type of support I needed as I continue to grow. The complete disregard for my growth journey and my life's vision probably would've led me to a breaking point and caused me to do the one thing I never want to do: head to divorce court. Luckily, I did the hard thing and left the relationship that could have made or broken my vision.

When a person can speak of lofty goals and a way to get there, then I know we're of the same mindset. Because I didn't have my milestones written out with a planned timetable attached to them, it took me too long to realize that the lofty goals he spoke of were just that—talk. It took me about a year and a half to realize I was making moves by leaps and bounds, and he was in the same place as when we started.

I'd lost many things, rebuilt my life, and continued to grow beyond what I originally lost in a short time. This gave him time to just exist. I was absorbed with starting over and building and hadn't noticed I was working alone. The combination of no support and lies to maintain a facade became unbearable for me. I was actively making my vision and dreams a reality. I thought we both were, but I realized that his dreams lived only in his head and I was expected to be part of a means of impressing others instead of building the blueprint for the life we really wanted to live.

This became glaringly evident when any opportunity to act or to take accountability came. He ran for the hills, and I was left to figure it out alone. After I realized we were going nowhere fast, I had to plan an exit strategy because I was determined not to get stuck pulling the weight of having ambition for two and trying to build with no support. I was already growing alone, so I needed to truly be alone to keep growing.

I was ready to go...then Covid happened. The nation declared a state of emergency with shelter in place. All my apartment walkthroughs were canceled. Property managers called and emailed that applications were on hold, and vacancies had been canceled because tenants decided to stay in place. I was forced to face the decisions that I had made for my life up to that point. Day after day, hour after hour, I was waiting to hear the news that we were finally rid of the seeming zombie apocalypse outside.

I decided to use my time wisely after we figured out that I couldn't leave the home. I did the hard work of owning every choice I made that led me to being locked inside the house with a person I had grown to loathe: every red flag I ignored, every conversation that proved we weren't on the same page, every unanswered question, and every milestone I didn't define in my own life. Had I written my vision and milestones and created my roadmap, I would've noticed far sooner that he didn't keep his promises and didn't intend to. I looked at myself and the gaps that made me susceptible to the string of bad decisions that ended with me locked inside an apartment in quarantine with a person who wasn't for me or my vision.

When I tell you it was hard, hard is an understatement. I shed many tears and prayed often, asking not only for forgiveness, but to be shown the hardest parts of both my head and heart to learn what I missed. I also repented for what I saw and ignored that led me to being physically stuck with this person. I chose not to play the victim and only held him accountable for the lies he told me. I also had to take ownership of my life and the things I shouldn't have released along the way. I had to learn better boundaries for myself.

If I had a healthier set of boundaries to begin with and had set my milestones with a timeline to achieve my vision, I would've gone in a different direction long before the onset of COVID-19. I was previously in a prison with the combination of all my decisions. But we don't know until we learn, and we have the option to use these difficult times to grow into a better version of ourselves. I chose to do the hard thing and win again.

My Lesson

The road isn't meant for me to travel alone the entire way, but it also isn't meant for me to travel with the wrong person. Knowing your vision and having milestones will help you in recognizing when a potential mate is simply repeating your vision back to you as opposed to sharing her actual vision. Such mirroring can be a device for someone to attach themselves to you for the wrong reasons. Pay attention when a potential partner can't articulate her life's vision to you or isn't accomplishing anything toward said vision without explanation over time. The life partner you choose is a large part of how successful you can become because that other person can serve as either an anchor or a weight.

You may ask what the difference is because an anchor does weigh down a ship, but an anchor serves a purpose: to keep the ship grounded when the ship's not supposed to move for a specific period, and it has a set weight that doesn't fluctuate. An anchor is a tool holding you in place when you need it and keeps you from going adrift before it's time for you to move along again. On the other hand, weight fluctuates, and excess weight can sink a ship. Once the ship sinks, it can't be recovered.

When your life partner is a weight, he isn't adding any value to your life or helping you build your vision. They're simply present. If we choose the wrong mate, he can sink our ship, or our growth can slow to a snail's crawl, and we can get used to being stagnant.

In dating, relationships, and marriage, the bond is much deeper than spending time with the same person every day. You spend a lot of your recharging hours with this person as well. You'll spend much of your time building, learning, and growing with him. If your partner isn't also growth-minded or at least committed to being a strong support system for you as you continue to build and grow (because he's already grown to full potential and wants to fulfill the remainder of his purpose by supporting you), then you may find yourself in a situation where he's weighing you down.

Sometimes, that weight may be hard to see because you have feelings for the person, and you may become distracted by the things he brings to the table. However, do those things serve your relationship and create a dynamic where you both can build each other? Note that it may not be what he brings to the table; it may just be your feelings that keep you enamored with a person who has no place in your vision or purpose.

When we aren't clear on our vision or haven't fully fleshed out bullet points for how to achieve it, we're more easily distracted by relationships that can hinder us. Similarly, when we only have the big picture in mind without mapping out milestones, we can be misguided into thinking that the wrong person will fit into that big picture. It takes time to recognize when we're being lied to. When we know our milestones, we can more easily tell that a potential life partner is ill-equipped for the job and won't grow to fill the needs on the way to our purpose and vision.

The biggest problem comes when you jump the gun and marry the person. For some, this may not seem like a big deal, but I'm speaking from a divorce-is-not-an-option perspective. I had to learn over time to choose wisely before I accepted who my life mate would be. I had to make hard decisions, including a lot of self-reflection, and own the fact that I had chosen the wrong people. I failed to realize that my life partner must be committed not only to me but to a growth mindset for me to get to my final vision. It can't be built with a mate who isn't willing to work with me or support me as I build toward my milestones brick by brick. This isn't solely based on financial support. There are mental, emotional, and spiritual aspects of supporting a partner's vision.

The person you choose or accept can be a blessing or a lesson. It's important to listen to the voice of God when making the final decision regarding your life partner with the intent to continue growing and building with one person for the rest of your life.

I won't go into divorce if this advice has come too late for you, because I'm not familiar with divorce and therefore can't speak on it. If that's where you are now, I encourage you to find qualified resources in people who can share their divorce experience so you can grow from there.

I decided I wouldn't live in shame for my mistake or carry guilt for freeing myself from a relationship that wasn't serving me, not building me in my purpose, leading me astray from my vision, and ultimately wasn't serving God. I encourage you to build a relationship that serves God as you live your everyday life. Both of you will combine your life visions and work together to accomplish your dreams and goals. There will be space for compromise that will benefit you both as you build and grow together over the long term.

But to be able to build together, you need a life partner who is willing to give 120% just as you do. When you're *both* striving to bring so much to the relationship, you can be confident that you can lean on one another when challenges come and tackle them together. Growing together looks different for each couple, but you can start by showing support, valuing each other, and filling gaps in each other's improvement areas.

<u>**Chapter 7 Go Notes:**</u>

- Your romantic partner is even more important than your platonic relationships because that person will influence the way you follow your vision roadmap. They'll help or harm the road to your vision.

- Don't choose your partner based on where you are now. Is the person a good fit for where you're going?

- Self-assess *before* you get involved in a romantic relationship. Intimately know your vision, purpose, and gaps. Know your qualities and non-negotiables regarding your partner.

- Let God have the final say on your potential relationship. If God says the person isn't a fit, don't move forward.

- Some of the top reasons for divorce are preventable:
  - Lack of communication
  - Constant arguing
  - Unrealistic expectations
  - Not being prepared for marriage
  - It all comes back to fully mapping out your vision with milestones (the big vision alone isn't enough; you need to be clear on both), managing your emotions and being understanding of your partner's feelings, and clearly communicating your boundaries.

<u>**Chapter 7 Action Exercises**</u>

1) At this point in the book, are you completely clear on your life's vision and milestones? If not, take time to finish writing those things out in detail in your journal.

2) Write a detailed inventory of the qualities you want in your life partner: the person's values, emotional behaviors, financial habits, your non-negotiables for the person, etc. When you're clear on the kind of partner you want, it's easier to spot the person if God puts them in your path (or vice versa).

   a) Who do *you* need to become to attract that person into your life? Get clear and honest, then add those milestones to your vision roadmap (if they're not already there).

8

JUST GO: CONQUERING A FEARFUL PATH

"Don't let light stealers dim the light God gave you. You have an authentic and natural light. There are some whose mission is to dim that light or extinguish that light. It's your job to let your light shine despite those efforts. You have a job to do..."

—Snappa Red, Extreme Execution Coach

When one of my personal development coaches said this to me on an accountability call, I thought to myself: "So go do it. Go be that light, no matter what. That's what I was designed for." I never considered that the same way I have a vision and purpose in life, someone else's purpose or mission could be to dim my light and make sure I don't fulfill what I was brought into this world to do. It never occurred to me that anyone would want to dim my light so that I wouldn't be able to make a positive impact on the world by encouraging people. I had only considered the good in the world, the God in the world, and never considered the other side of the coin. Just as there is goodness in the world, there is evil, and it seems that one may not exist without the other.

I like to think of everyone as good, but there can be some unsavory circumstances or ignorance that can lead us to do things that may hurt other people or hurt us and lead us to stray from our life's vision. I believe God still uses these things to teach us lessons and prepare us for the life we're supposed to have as long as we remain Birthaful and continue to grow and work for the goals that we've set out to accomplish for ourselves.

We may encounter roadblocks or people who discourage us from continuing to achieve our ultimate purpose at the end, but the encounters we consider negative are exactly what we need to show us that we're on the right path and going in the right direction on that path. Though we always try to take the path of least resistance, if there are no challenges on the path, then the path isn't right. If the path is clear and easy to travel, then everyone would go.

Some people are a part of your obstacles. When the wrong people are in your presence or even stumble upon you, it's your job to let your light shine despite their best efforts to dim it. There will always be people against you, but that doesn't mean you have to let them win, even when those who are against you used to be your best friend, a romantic partner, or even a family member.

It's not always your job to bring someone a message or let them know of the open door(s) available. There are times when the open doors aren't even meant for the people you're encouraging to enter them, especially when they're not prepared for it. You can't act as God. The decision isn't yours to push them to greatness. You can only make that decision for yourself and encourage others to make their best life. We're not all on the same schedule. The timelines of our lives may converge at one point or another, but that doesn't mean we're all meant to stay together for life. When someone's breakthrough is in the breakdown, and you continue to save them, you're in the way of God's work. Whether you do it knowingly or *un*knowingly, you're blocking your blessing and that of the other person.

“One sows, one
waters…”

It may be one person's job to sow seeds into your life and another person's job to water them. Another person comes into your life to tend the plant, and yet another to pick the fruit. We need others in our circle, but we need the right ones in our circle. Respect the reason and the season for allowing others to come and go. Just as others are meant to help you, you're also meant to help others for the proper reason or in the proper season.

Think of how you can help to sow, tend, water, or pick the fruit in someone else's life. If you don't fit any of those roles, then you need to *move*, get out of the way, or get *into* position. Remembering this empowers you to let the right people in, to let the wrong people go, and to know when you're truly helping cultivate a reciprocal relationship. Either way, you have a specific place and time to be someone else's seasonal help. Don't overstay, because that means you're not in position for your next task, which will cause a breakdown or failure in the next place you're supposed to be. Get to your next level.

When the time comes for you to be in isolation, don't waste that time. Use that isolation to your advantage to strategize and come up with a plan for what you want to do next in your life. Spend time with God and listen to His voice for guiding you through that season of isolation. It won't last forever, but you can cause the season to be longer than it has to be.

There are things you're meant to learn while you rest in this time alone. And while you're alone, there will be times when you are afraid to move forward without anyone else by your side. I greatly encourage you to go ahead and do it anyway, especially that thing that scares you the most. Be afraid if that's the emotion you're feeling, but do it anyway. When you're unsure of your direction or the outcomes, refer to your milestones. You've already created your roadmap, so even if you become lost, you don't have to stay lost.

You've written down the directions to guide you, you know the next direction you're headed in, you just have to grow towards how to get there.

"*Get ready, stay ready. Prepare yourself. Activate yourself. It's not a question of 'if'. A fall is coming. Do the work to be prepared for the fall.*"

—Ashling Cole

An accountability coach of mine, Ashling, had been exercising and stretching on a regular basis for optimal health and fitness. During her walk, she took a tumble. She fell forward and caught herself in a pushup position—the same stance she dropped into each morning during her workout regime day after day. Muscle memory kicked in, and she was able to catch herself as opposed to injuring herself during the fall. She shared that if she'd taken the same fall just one year earlier—before her fitness journey began—she wouldn't've had the reflexes or the strength to catch herself and leave the fall safely.

The same goes for us. We have to prepare before a fall comes so that we naturally know what to do, in some cases without even consciously *thinking* of what to do. This is why it's so important to continuously work on ourselves and revisit the areas where we believe we've already conquered our bad habits or tendencies. Keeping the wrong people is one of those things. To respect the reason, the season, or the lifetime, we must do maintenance work and take inventory of the self-improvements we've made so we can build upon them. We must review all those improvements at every level until we've truly mastered the art of becoming our new selves. There will be some spaces in which we'll make permanent and lasting change in our lives, but there are other habits that we'll have to conquer repeatedly to live the life we've dreamed of.

My Own Story: Writing This Book

One Friday at the end of the first calendar quarter, I decided to announce to my accountability group that I would finally be writing this book. I did this so I would actually write it. After living these experiences for 20-plus years, after deciding I would be brave and share my story to help others, and after much thought on what my second quarter goal would be, I proclaimed I would do this.

I never thought that by making that commitment both in my heart and aloud to my beloved group of 25 or so people that I would be tested just two days later. That I would have to take my own advice and teachings and put them to practice yet again without delaying, without procrastinating, without lingering around too long, without *moving* when I received the directive to move, while being afraid of the next door to the next room but doing it anyway.

I received the news that my beloved accountability group would be no more and that there would be a transition to a new level. There was a new opportunity at five to 10 times the cost. My problem wasn't that *I* couldn't go—in fact, I had nothing but my decision in the way of me going. The problem was I had to get comfortable with the uncomfortable and accept that all the familiar faces I came to love and care for wouldn't be waiting for me in the next place.

All the opportunities I received from this group over the years did exactly what they were supposed to: elevate me, level me up, strengthen my Birtha, and improve my finances, pushing me further in trusting new people and showing me that reciprocal relationships are real, and I can have them! With them, I learned to become a better family leader (of the family I was born into so that I could be strong yet submissive in the family that will be born from me); they held me accountable for being fit, taking care of myself, and growing into the best version of myself.

Even with all those lessons, I wasn't taught to not have the emotions that come with leaving one space and group to continue the pursuit of my dreams. I wasn't encouraged to bury those negative feelings. Instead, I was taught to embrace those feelings and *grow* through them, not go through them.

By closing that chapter of life and embracing all that I was taught, able to give, and gained in that space, I must again accept that everybody can't go. I have to process the difficult truths that I've laid out for you in this book and move forward with the opportunity presented for me, along with others who have done the work and are prepared to go, too. There's no love lost for anyone who's not ready to make this next level, and I hope everyone I dearly care for feels the same.

I know what my vision is—the milestones I mapped out and the goals I set—so I must keep going. I accept that all my seasons aren't always as I wish them to be or in alignment with everyone else's. I respect that some familiar faces were in my life for a reason, and that was fulfilled. It's not my place to push boundaries or pull people along in places where no one has asked for my input on the matter. My responsibility is to be a truth-telling author, one who lives by what I've written, with hopes that I've empowered you.

With great humility and a twinge of fear at not knowing what's behind the next door or who will be in the next room, I can't remain stagnant. I must keep growing through things beyond my control while remembering, accepting, and respecting that Everybody Can't Go.

<u>**Chapter 8 Go Notes**</u>

- Understand that some people's purpose in your life is to dim your light. There are good and evil purposes in this world. Stay focused.

- People may be in your life for a season, and the same may be true for your role in their lives as well.

- Embrace your seasons of isolation, and don't waste that time. You have your roadmap with its milestones, so continue on your path. If you're feeling afraid, that's okay. Do it anyway.
- When someone's breakthrough is in the breakdown, and you continue to save them, you're in the way of God's work. Whether you do it knowingly or *un*knowingly, you're blocking your blessing and that of the other person.

<u>**Chapter 8 Action Exercises**</u>

1) Reflect on your role in your relationships and other people's role in your life. Do you sow, water, tend, or reap? What role(s) do people play in your life?

Noting this will help you better navigate your relationships going forward. Remember, if your answer is none of the above, then you need to *move*, get out of the way, or get *into* position.

This will help you let the right people in and let the wrong people go.

2) Constantly work on self-improvement. As Ashling Cole said, a fall is coming. It's better to be prepared for it.

Writing Out Your Vision & Roadmap Just Got Easier.

Get your copy of the companion book, *Write the Vision, Make it Plain: an Everybody Can't Go Journal*, **today**.

Carve out your vision and make life-changing break-throughs in the journal as you work through this book.

Available now on Amazon.com: https://a.co/d/1njlUPw

CONCLUSION/CLOSING

Congratulations, friend. In reading and working through this book, you've done what 99% of the world *won't* do. In a recent study, only 1% of the world's population does their soul work: self-assessment, creating a vision and roadmap, taking inventory of the people and habits that no longer serve them, creating healthy boundaries, having the hard but necessary conversations, fully grieving their losses, seeking spiritual development, and surrounding themselves with people who will push them closer to their goal while offering them the chance to be mutually beneficial.

You're in the 1% now.

Let that sink in.

You're one of 80 million people—*worldwide*—who chose to do your deep work. This puts you way ahead of the game. I applaud you for valuing yourself, your vision, your purpose, and your well-being. When you're healed, whole, clear, and focused, you're unstoppable in God's hands.

So, what's next?

The last tool I'll leave you with is one I briefly mentioned in Chapter 2. I referred to four human behavior styles and shared that we all usually have one or two dominant ones and need to create relationships with those who complement our less dominant ones. The **Extreme Execution Flight Assessment 2.0**, an easy-to-understand version of the DISC Assessment, is a game-changer. It's not a test, so don't worry about right or wrong answers. Just answer each question honestly based on who you are and how you behave right now.

This assessment will not only give you a powerful snapshot of who you are right now, but you'll also receive a comprehensive 19-page report detailing:

a) your dominant behavior style(s) and natural strengths
b) your less dominant styles
c) tips on how to use your strengths to your advantage
d) tips on how to complement your less dominant styles
e) most importantly, tips on how others should treat *you* based on your natural strengths and limitations

For a minimal cost and just 15 minutes of your time, you'll gain the rare, unfair advantage of quickly learning how people tick as you meet or speak to them, which you get to keep for the rest of your life. You'll also gain cheat codes for creating better relationships and spotting mutually beneficial opportunities.

Most importantly, this tool will save you time, money, and heartache by helping you learn who you need in your life and who **can't go.**

This assessment will give you even more context for completing the action steps laid out at the end of each chapter in this book. When you complete your assessment and get the results, hit me up so we can walk you through the next steps to make the most of what you've learned.

Send me a message directly at **<u>Info@EverybodyCG.com</u>** to take your assessment, get a clear picture of who you are, and gain even greater ground on the path to completing your vision.

ACKNOWLEDGEMENTS

Everybody Can't Go, the book that became the brand and now a movement has been a long time coming. The manuscript journey that began several years ago, took on a life of its own as I continued to learn, grow and level up. Even though everybody didn't make it with me to this point, there were so many true friends, mentors and people who poured into me as this project grew far beyond just a book.

First and foremost, thank God for the vision to share my story and what I've learned that can help others as they work through friendship breakups, romantic breakups and setting hard boundaries with family and others on their own journey.

To my Breathe University (BU) and Eric Thomas University (ETU) coaches: Ashling, Commish, Darrick (Innanet Dad), Derek (DLo), Snappa Red, Tarnissha and Tyrus; thank you for pushing me daily through several transitions and stages of my personal level up; letting me know when I needed to pick up the pace or when I was going too hard on myself in the pursuit of perfection.

For putting me in the hot seat and pushing me to the heights of making Everybody Can't Go into an entire brand offering a suite of products and services, your coaching on writing and book development, thank you Brandon Burns (BranBear).

For editing my manuscript, being my writing coach, letting me talk you into crazy things and always answering to listen to my chatter, thank you Mellissa Thomas (Mell T).

For being a community to me on a whole new level, with acceptance, love, encouragement and sharpening me once I had gone through the fire of loss, grieving, learning in isolation and rebuilding; I am grateful that I became an individual that you all could embrace and consider me family. Thank you to my entire You Owe You Mastermind family.

LDH, Mignon, Moose, and Wedzere thank you for your continued support, encouragement and guidance as my book and brand developed from my small idea to the blueprint for a way to impact the world.

For being obedient to God's calling over your life and changing my life before we'd ever shaken hands. For creating the rooms that have connected me to people that have influenced change in me for better than I could have ever imagined spiritually, in self growth, mutual relationships, and support, thank you Dr. Eric Thomas (ET).

For making ET and his message accessible in a way that I could find him online and begin to grow before I had a dime to participate in-person. For not letting me give up, making me move past my own potential and being a real life demonstration of what that growth looks like in real time thank you Karl Phillips (Big Neff Karl).

Thank you to the relationships and friendships that had to end as their season was over and I am grateful for the lessons learned as a result of what each of you brought to my life during your season.

www.ingramcontent.com/pod-product-compliance
Lightning Source LLC
Chambersburg PA
CBHW050733150726
48196CB00038B/909/J